THE TROUT BOOK

A Complete Angler's Guide

by

Frank Sargeant

Book IV in the Inshore Library

by Larsen's Outdoor Publishing

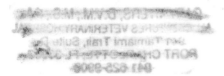

Copyright ©1992 by Frank Sargeant

ISBN 0-936513-21-7

Library of Congress 92-071318

Published by:

LARSEN'S OUTDOOR PUBLISHING
2640 Elizabeth Place
Lakeland, FL 33813

PRINTED IN THE UNITED STATES OF AMERICA

3 4 5 6 7 8 9 10

2

ACKNOWLEDGEMENTS

It takes a lot of help to write a book. I've been blessed with the help of dozens of good friends, guides, outstanding anglers, biologists and more in producing this book, as in all the others of the Inshore Library series. Some who were particularly helpful in THE TROUT BOOK were Gene Lechler and Mike Locklear at Homosassa, Frank Schiraldi at Crystal River, Dennis Royston and Everett Antrim at Tarpon Springs, David Fairbanks, Paul Hawkins, Russ Sirmons, James Wood and Jim O'Neal at Tampa Bay, Scott Moore, Bill Miller, Larry Mendez and Pete Greenan at Charlotte Harbor, Doug Bird at the Laguna Madre in Texas, and Ronny Groinier and Terry Shaughnessy in the bayou country of Louisiana. DNR biologist Mike Murphy was also a great help in the trout habits and habitat section, and the engineers at Outboard Marine Corporation, Stratos, Hydra-Sports and at Bob's Machine were helpful in the chapter on rigging and running boats for the flats.

COVER: The cover illustration of a battling sea trout was sculpted in glass by St. Petersburg artist and guide Russ Sirmons. Sirmons cuts these remarkable works into thick glass plates with sandblasting equipment, taking weeks to perfect a single piece. He accepts commissions to do fish and birds of all species. His telephone number is (813) 526-2090.

3

PREFACE

Seatrout fishing is a sport in transition, changing rapidly from a "meat" fishery to a sporting pursuit. The changes are not only because of the general change in concern and temperament among anglers, but because habitat problems and overharvest in many areas require the change. Size limits, lower daily bags, reduction of commercial harvests and other controls will necessarily be a part of the future of trout fishing throughout the range of the species.

THE TROUT BOOK approaches seatrout fishing on two fronts. One is to point out how anglers can improve their skills to take advantage of fisheries that have declined a bit from historic highs, fisheries that hopefully are in transition as well, on the way back instead of on the way out, as they should be with wise management.

Secondly, THE TROUT BOOK points out those areas where it's still "the good old days"--areas where the changes in habitat and the growing population have done little damage to fish numbers. Fortunately, there are still many of these, and thanks to the help of expert anglers, guides and biologists throughout the southeast, we've been able to pack many of them within these covers.

THE TROUT BOOK can be of assistance whether you're a complete beginner or a gray-bearded old salt with fish scales stuck in your whiskers, because the chapters range from the basic to the esoteric, the locales from your own backyard to the most distant habitats of the species.

THE TROUT BOOK can get you started, but don't overlook the one most important chapter, the one that lists the phone numbers of the many guides who really wrote this book. A day in their company can make a trout fisherman of

5

you. Take advantage of their expertise--you'll find many of them able to impart wisdom beyond the simple loading of the fish box, and willing to provide you with insights into method, habitat and conservation that you will carry with you long after the day on the water. It's a great value at a moderate price.

CONTENTS

ABOUT THE AUTHOR

Frank Sargeant is outdoors editor of the Tampa Tribune and one of America's best-known outdoor writers. He holds a masters degree in English and Creative Writing from Ohio University and has taught writing at the high school and college level. He was formerly an editor for CBS Publications and a writer for Disney World Publications, as well as southern editor for Outdoor Life. Sargeant's award-wining articles and photos have also appeared regularly in Sports Afield, Outdoor Life, Southern Outdoors, Southern Saltwater and BassMaster. He fished with dozens of trout guides throughout the southeast in compiling this, the fourth volume in his Inshore Library Series. He is also author of THE SNOOK BOOK, THE REDFISH BOOK and THE TARPON BOOK. Sargeant lives on the Little Manatee River near Tampa, Florida.

CHAPTER 1

INTRODUCTION:
THE SPOTTED SEATROUT

It's the trout that's not a trout.

Spotted seatrout, Cynoscion nebulosus, are not trout at all, of course. They come from a less distinguished family, the croakers, the noise-making toads of fishdom; an across-the-tracks lineage if ever there was one.

But they are perhaps stepchildren in that family. They look not at all like toads, nor even like black drum. They have the streamlined beauty and iridescent, silver-purple glow of the cold-water salmonids, the Cinderella fish. They're also favored with the same sort of beauty marks found on freshwater brown trout, the bold spots across the back and the fins that earn them their name. Or at least, one of their names. They're also called specks, spotted weakfish, spotted squeteague, and most commonly, just plain "trout".

Whatever you call them, they are the most popular of all saltwater fish throughout most of their range. This is the result both of their abundance and their cooperative nature-- trout are the panfish of the sea, always willing to grab a bait or a lure, usually not too difficult to find, and wonderful in the pan--yet they display an aggressive nature and a willingness to wallop topwater plugs that mark them as true gamefish.

Trout - The Family Fish

Trout are family fish, the first fish of many budding sportsmen, not demanding great expertise in rigging tackle or making delicate and distant presentations--though those who

Cynoscion nebulosus, the spotted seatrout, is a resident of estuaries from Mexico to Chesapeake Bay, and is the nation's most popular inshore gamefish. The species can survive water temperatures in the lower 50's, but their northern range is limited by extended cold weather.

study the trout fishing arts will find there's much to know, lots of room for growth with study and experience.

They don't require great strength or skill to land. They're not the biggest or the strongest of fish, not long-running nor high-jumping nor deep-diving. And yet many anglers have a special affection for trout. They are as dependable as old friends, as comfortable as worn shoes, as welcoming as country roads. Trout fishing is an undemanding pursuit that offers only pleasure and relaxation--rather than an ego trip--in the catching.

Broad Ranging Homebodies

And trout are found in protected inshore waters that can be reached in the smallest of boats on most days--and in water so shallow that no boat at all is needed many times. Trout are a fish made for the wade fisherman and the bridge patrol, and their home waters are often the clear, shallow grass flats, those wonderful windows into the edge of the sea that are a blessing to the eye and to the soul.

They're also found, at varying times, in the rolling surf off the open Gulf, in grimy ship basins in the heart of industrialized

Trout readily take a wide variety of artificial plugs, jigs and spoons as well as many small live baits. They can also be taken on flyrod poppers and streamers as shown here.

ports, and far up coastal rivers in waters that are almost completely fresh. Anywhere you choose to go down to the sea in the southeast, the trout will meet you there.

Seatrout are, it can't be denied, members of the croaker family, so-called because they can produce a croaking or drumming sound by vibrating their swim bladders. Their closest relatives are the weakfish, found in the waters of the mid-Atlantic coast, and the silver seatrout, found throughout southeastern coastal waters of the U.S. Their body shapes are nearly identical to both, though their vivid spots distinguish them.

Their body coloration can vary hugely, with fish bright as silver dollars taken from clear water along the beaches of the Gulf, and fish dark as black bass showing up far up coastal rivers in late winter. They are also distinguished by their bright yellow mouths, particularly in spawning time, and by the twin canine teeth located top-center in their mouths.

The range is large, extending from Chesapeake Bay south to the tip of Florida's Everglades, then around the sweep of the Gulf as far south as Campeche, Mexico. They're most abundant from Georgia south and west, however, and are found in inshore waters year around south of the Georgia/Florida line. Most never leave their home estuaries throughout their lives.

13

The great thing about fishing trout in all that stretch of country is that you can go at it on your own level and still expect reasonable success. If you're happy plunking a shrimp out there, sipping a cold one and waiting for something to happen, you can do that in a lot of places and expect success.

If you're a topwater fanatic, trout are made for floaters. If you like spider-webby 2-pound-test lines, trout are great fish to test your skill--and empty your tacklebox. And if you take pleasure in the rhythm and flow of fly-casting, trout will happily swallow your streamer or belt your bug.

In short, seatrout are the sea's gift to the common man. We have, unfortunately, treated them somewhat too commonly in some areas until recent years, and delicate creatures that they are, they've responded by disappearing from many traditional haunts, or reducing their numbers in others thanks to a combination of water degradation and overfishing.

On the upside, however, most states are now serious about stopping destruction of seagrass beds and mangrove habitats and also working to prevent excessive nutrient from entering their estuaries. Dredge and fill is controlled, if not stopped, and habitat mitigation--the replanting of sea grasses and creation of new estuarine areas--is a growing art.

Finally, the recreational catch is now being limited throughout trout range, and commercial net harvest is rapidly being phased out--as it must be if numbers are ever to return. If all these good intentions bear fruit, the fishing future looks as bright as the silver side of a searun trout.

CHAPTER 2

TROUT SMARTS

Some guys just seem to instinctively know where trout are going to be.

And some of us couldn't find one if we were ushered into the National Seatrout Convention and given front row seats.

Those gurus who always know are despicable. They carry in their wallets photos of whole strings of trout which you would kill simply to catch one of in your lifetime.

"See 'at one there that wouldn't fit in a hunnert quart Igloo?" they'll chortle. "We got 40 like 'at 'un in three hours."

Sure enough, there the obscene monster lies, head out one end of the cooler, tail out the other. Usually they pull these photos out when your wife is around.

"Isn't that something," she'll say. "Frank hasn't caught a keeper in six months. I thought you said the trout were all gone, Honey."

These guys probably cheat at golf, too. Don't speak to them, or nod at them when they pass in their boats.

Unless they invite you to go along, of course, or if you think they might.

Other than getting the Received Word from a trout guru, there are ways of finding trout with some consistency, however.

Trout are creatures of habit, not much given to long migrations. Most are born, live and die within five miles of the same blade of grass. This probably makes them horrible bores at cocktail parties, but makes it reasonably easy to find a trout when you want one, which, if you're like me, you mostly do.

The secret of finding trout is much like the secret of finding good real estate, location, location and location. Or in the case of trout, habitat, habitat and habitat. More than any other inshore gamefish, trout are intimately connected to the sea grasses that make up the primary habitat of the coastal flats. For most of the year in most areas, find the grass and you find the fish.

In some areas, grass patches are scarce and obvious, and it's no problem to find the trout which have no choice but to make use of them for cover. The patches along the southeast shore of Florida's Tampa Bay are an example as this is written-- they are the remnants of once vast grass beds, and water quality improvements are restoring them, but there's still lots of white, bare sand between each oblong swath of grass, particularly as you approach water deeper than 4 feet. Not surprisingly, throughout the temperate months, each of these patches is good for a couple of nice trout.

Trout relate to many types of grass, but the most productive vegetation in most areas is what is known as "turtle grass", which looks much like eel grass in fresh water, with flat-bladed strands that can reach lengths of over two feet in deep, clear water.

Turtle grass has a special appeal to trout, perhaps because of its depth and the considerable escape cover it offers, as well as being an attractant for shrimp, crabs and small baitfish of all kinds. Trout are given to hiding when a predator approaches rather than taking off at high speed as pelagic species do, which is why their backs have evolved to the olive green, mottled pattern they wear. When a trout settles down on bottom in a stand of turtle grass, it's very hard to see from overhead, even if you know exactly where to look.

Trout can also be found in other types of bottom vegetation, including what some people call sea lettuce, wigeon grass and roll grass, but none of these hold fish in the numbers or with the consistency of turtle grass. So step one in most areas is finding large expanses of turtle grass.

Of course, in some areas you can find too much. Vast fields of grass like those in Mosquito Lagoon on Florida's east coast or off Homosassa on the west, or on the back side of the Chandeleurs in Louisiana or in the Laguna Madre in Texas

Trout experts like David Fairbanks, five-time IGFA world-line-class record holder, seem to instinctively know where to find trout. Getting on fish consistently is a matter of understanding their habitat needs, food requirements and seasonal movements, Fairbanks and other pros say.

look great and are clear evidence of fine trout populations-- but some areas of the grass produce and a whole lot don't. When you have limited time, sorting out which areas to work on can be a problem--which is why it's a good idea to hire a guide the first time you visit a new area.

But free-lancing a new area is fun on your own, and if you learn the basics of what trout seek in a home, you can usually find fish.

Getting An Edge

Trout, like both other fish and shorebound wildlife, seem to prefer "edge" cover, the point at which one type of habitat meets another. Probably this offers feeding variety, or perhaps it's an easy geographic mark for the fish to home on, but in any case, if you find one of these cover breaks, work it carefully.

The break may be the point where a shallow grass flat suddenly drops off to deeper grass, depth increasing from a foot to three or four. (Note that this is not a big drop--and sometimes an increase in depth of only a foot can be enough to key a trout-gathering spot. One of the interesting aspects of hunting trout is learning to be alert for these subtle clues.)

Or it might be the point where the grass meets hard shell bottom. Or where the grass is cut by a tidal channel.

It can sometimes be where the turtle grass runs out and another type of grass begins. Or it can be where the bottom

17

has been scoured clean by strong tide flows, leaving bare sand adjoining thick grass. Maybe it's a remote rockpile in the middle of acres of sand bottom. It can be a wrecked boat, or a reef outcrop along a beach.

Whatever, when you spot one of these zones, explore it carefully. Very often, edges produce.

Water Color

There's also such a thing as the "right" color for trout water. The experts know this color, without being able to describe it.

Good trout water is not too clear, maybe because it makes the fish too vulnerable to ospreys and other fisheaters. It's not too murky--brown, muddy water turns off trout in most areas. (An exception is the Georgia/South Carolina coast, but even there, the fish bite best when the water is relatively clearer than its normal too-thin-to-plow condition.)

Just the right shade is a milky green, with visibility of about 4 to 8 feet, which is to say you can just make out the variations in bottom grass and sand from the boat as you pass over those depths. Find an edge in prime habitat with this water color and visibility and you're 90 percent of the way home.

Interestingly, changes in water color can function as an edge. I've often seen trout school up at the break where a dark coastal river flows into the clearer water of the Gulf, or where the muds created by porpoises on a flat meet the clearer surrounding water. Apparently the trout make use of the mud as cover, picking off bait that comes down the break line.

The classic example of this behavior comes along Florida's west coast during the spring and fall shrimp migration, when not only trout but grunts, mackerel, seabass, grouper and a bit of everything else go on the prowl for the crustaceans, pursuing them with such vigor that they create "muds" that may be a mile wide and two miles long. More about this in the Homosassa chapter, but suffice it to say, any area where water color changes abruptly is worth your close attention.

Finding a "Bite"

For consistent angling action on trout, it's best to learn waters close to home, and learn them well. But there's no

Fishing the right lure in the right place at the right time results in catches like this, taken in the Louisiana delta country. (Photo by Larry Larsen.)

question that at certain times in certain places, trout go bonkers. The grass really is greener in these areas at these times, and it behooves you now and then to hitch up the boat trailer and go off to the distant hotspot for a day when everything is just right there.

How do you know when to go where?

This is why God created newspaper fishing writers, silly. Or silly newspaper fishing writers, as you will.

Anyway, go down to your local news stand and buy a Friday newspaper from the area that interests you. There, somewhere in the sports pages, will be the week's fishing report.

Many times they list the fish camps giving the report, and some of these camp owners have been known on occasion to actually tell the truth, at least when the fish are biting. Most camp owners are optimists, but not outright liars--if they say trout fishing is fair, it stinks. If they say it's good, it's not too bad. If they say it's great, it might be worth a trip. If they say it's the best in 20 years and they've got pictures to prove it, load up--there's a bite going on.

These bonanzas are usually related to an explosion in the food supply. For example, in Florida the finger mullet migration into the bays of the east coast drives trout (and lots of other fish) nuts from late September to the end of October. The aforementioned shrimp movements do the job about 4 to

Scot Brantley, former NFL linebacker, is among the elite inshore anglers who always seem to know where the trout will bite. This one was taken at Charlotte Harbor.

8 miles off Chassahowitzka, Homosassa and Crystal River on Florida's west coast in April and November. Whitebait or scaled sardines attract lots of fish to the rockpiles off Hudson and Hernando Beach in August and September, and guide Jim Bradley says hundred-fish days are still a possibility there during that flurry.

The Steinhatchee and the Suwannee rivers, among others, have remarkable trout migrations on the first cold fronts of December. And the shrimp coming out of the Apalachicola delta in November account for enormous catches in the bay itself, and in the creeks and bayous north of the U.S. 98 Causeway. In the days before limits, many boats came back to the docks with 150 or more trout from this aggregation.

Many areas of the coast have similarly golden moments, most short-lived and localized--the Georgia coast has a great surge in late October. Get there on the peak and you'll experience fishing like the good old days.

Of course, you can't keep all the fish now like you could then. But take pictures. Keep them in your wallet, ready to whip out next time that trout guru comes around.

CHAPTER 3

TOPWATER TROUT

Shlurp, gurgle, pop, glub, bloop.

Can you speak topwater?

If you can't, you're missing a bet in most Southern waters when it comes to shallow water fishing for trout and redfish. It's probably safe to say that fewer than 5 percent of the catch of both species is taken on topwaters, but that's only because most anglers don't make use of these versatile lures.

There are times when topwaters will outfish plastic-tailed jigs--probably the universal favorite for both species--by a mile. There are even times--and I've seen plenty of them-- when floating lures will outfish live baits.

To be sure, there are also times when you can't buy a bite on a topwater, no matter what you do, while a well-placed jig or a sinking plug is cleaning house. But in the right place, at the right time--and fished in the right way--the topwater is an awesome weapon.

There's an understandable reluctance to use topwaters, because they skip along on the edge of the trout's environment, instead of plummeting down to where he lives. Logic says that a sinking lure ought to do better.

But when fish are in shallow water--and trout are noted for their love of yard-deep grass flats, sand bars and shell reefs--the topwater is easy for them to see and close enough so that they don't have to go out of their way to hit.

More importantly, it doesn't spend half of each cast buried in the grass where they can't find it, or snagged on shells where you can't retrieve it. And because it floats, you don't have to move it rapidly to keep it from snagging--you can let

21

it sit within inches of an oyster bar, bobbing and wiggling enticingly until any nearby fish just can't stand it.

It's been my experience that you often catch bigger fish with topwaters than with sinking baits such as jigs or live shrimp, particularly in spring, when spawning trout prowl the flats, and in fall and warm periods of winter. The reason, I suspect, is that juveniles feed primarily on shrimp--which a jig imitates--while adults eat primarily baitfish like mullet, pinfish and sardines. Topwaters imitate baitfish.

Find The Bait

The lures work best in areas where baitfish are likely to be found--in fact, one trick for finding big trout is to run the edges of the flats until you spot jumping mullet or pods of sardines rippling at the surface. If you stop and drift around the bait, casting flashy topwater lures, you'll find action sooner or later.

On falling tides, when the pull of the current draws out hundreds of finger mullet and other bait into the deeper channels, fish creek mouths and the sloughs that come out of small bays into larger ones, or out of small creeks into larger saltwater rivers.

Also, check out oyster bars as the water just begins to fall off of them--as it goes, all the small fish and crabs that have been safe on top will have to come back into deeper water where trout are likely to be cruising.

The trick in these areas is to cast a topwater well up into the shallow water--which may be only inches deep--and bring it dancing back over the drop-off.

Topwater Designs

A jig is a jig is a jig--there's not a whole lot of difference between most brands. But topwaters require a bit more sophistication in design. Some that work great for one species won't draw a look from others. And there are even individual differences in action between lures that appear to be identical in every way. Every experienced topwater angler has a few battle-scarred veteran lures that he wouldn't trade for your best bird dog, because he knows that something about those particular lures rings the bell--and a lot of others don't.

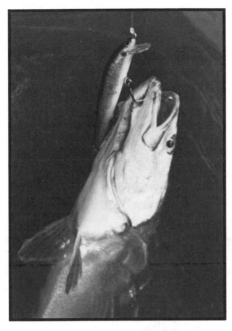

Topwaters like the Bangolure SP-5 are deadly when trout are found on shallow grass flats. The lures are worked with sharp twitches of the rod, rather than being activated by the reel.

Buy several of the models you like and sort through them to find that "sweet" one that is perfect. Then, guard it with your life. Go in there with the skeeters to get it back when it lands in the mangroves. Don't throw it in front of jacks or mackerel. Wash it off after each use.

Sleep with it under your pillow. Perfect lures are hard to find.

Everybody has their favorites. My own are the 5M MirrOlure--silver sides, green, black or blue back, and the SP-5 Bangolure--silver with a black back or Tennessee shad finish. Both have spinners to create extra splash when you jerk the line--essential in saltwater, where you need something to attract a fish's attention, even in choppy water. The Bangolure has a plastic lip, which makes it dive and flash sideways when you pull the line--deadly action. With the MirrOlure, there are spinners on both the front and the back. Many anglers remove the front spinner, because it tends to twist the line around its shaft--the back spinner provides plenty of attraction by itself, and the slight change in balance caused by removing the front spinner seems to give the lure a better sound in the water.

Other topwaters that catch lots of trout are the Devil's Horse, the 95M MirrOlure and the Torpedo. The venerable Zara Spook is a long-time favorite, as well, as is the Dalton Special. All of these are large, noisy baits that work best when the water is fairly rough. They're also good big-fish plugs.

The 28M MirrOlure is just about unbeatable in late spring and throughout the summer when the scaled sardine or "white bait" run is on. It's just the right size--but the larger 7M is also effective, and is probably a better bait where finger mullet, rather than sardines, are the favorite food for big trout. The floating Rat-L-Trap is also good when sardines or threadfins are the hot bait.

A new bait for big trout is the soft-plastic floater such as the floating jig from 12-Fathom and the Culprit Jerk Worm. These look a lot like needlefish, and they're single-hook lures, which makes them good when floating weeds make it impossible to fish treble-hook plugs.

The Rhythm Method

Each lure does best when fished in a particular way--but all are manipulated with the rod, rather than the reel. With floater-divers like the Bango, the best action is usually created by a short, sharp twitch of the rod, which causes the nose to dig in and the bait to dart sideways as the tail spinner sends out an attractive "schlurp".

Immediately after the twitch, it's essential to let the rod tip drift back toward the lure several inches, allowing slight line slack, so that the lure pops back up only a few inches from where it went down, instead of staying down and jumping forward. Slack is then taken up with the reel and the movement repeated.

With lures that stay on top--the MirrOlure, Devil's Horse, Jerk Worm and Tiny Torpedo--there's no need to give slack, but still the twitches should be imparted with short, sharp wrist action to the rod. Hesitate after each twitch before you take in line--the strikes usually come as the lure sits motionless.

With the Zara Spook and the 95M MirrOlure, you "walk the dog" by constantly twitching the rod tip back and forth,

Big trout are inclined to take topwater plugs because they are primarily fish eaters. The largest fish don't hesitate to grab a big mouthful, so large, noisy plugs sometimes do the job.

allowing an instant of slack between each twitch, as you reel steadily. This makes the lure dance back and forth in a zig-zag that draws some incredible strikes. It's tiring on the wrists, but a good way to cover lots of water in a hurry.

Topwater Tricks

Some people don't like to fish topwaters because they get lots of strikes but don't hook many fish. This can be corrected, usually, by slowing the lure down. Many times a trout makes a rush at a topwater, creating a huge boil, but turning away at the last instant. He doesn't go far away after this, though. If you let the lure sit a moment, then begin to just barely twitch and wiggle it, the fish will often come back.

If trout roll at the plug but don't take it, it may be too big to suit them. Go to a smaller lure, or add a trailer jig. The trailer hangs on a dropper or short leader attached to the back of the lure. Most use about 18 inches of mono with a 1/8 ounce bucktail or plastic-tailed jig. Fish rise to the surface disturbance, then spot the jig and suck it in if they decide not to go after the larger floating lure. Use fairly heavy leader material--about 30-pound-test--between the plug and the jig.

It's stiff enough to prevent frequently looping and tangling with the plug's trebles.

The "Drop" Spook from Heddon is designed just for this type of fishing, with a hole down the length of the plug so that you can run your line through the lure and out the back to tie it on to a jig. When a fish rolls at the plug but doesn't take, you give a bit of slack and the jig drops right in front of their nose-- few can resist.

Go Long

You'll do best on topwaters if you can make lengthy casts-- fish often see the boat when they follow a lure in close. Easiest way to extend your casting distance is use a longer rod--I added 30 feet to my range by switching to Berkley's B50-7M Series One graphites, seven-foot, two-handers with very stiff shafts but extremely light weight. Other builders make similar sticks. Match the rod with a light-weight reel like the new Shimano Calcutta, spooled with 10-pound test and you'll get remarkable distance, even with relatively light wood lures.

It's necessary to use a bit of extra caution in boat handling when fishing topwaters, too. Best approach is via electric trolling motor or push pole--fish won't hold in shallow water if you run your big outboard anywhere near them, even at idle speed. In fact, many anglers opt for slipping over the side and wade-fishing, which greatly lowers their profile and usually adds a lot to the catch, once they locate an area where fish are gathered.

The best times of day for topwaters are low light periods-- dawn, dusk and dark, plus on cloudy days. You'll occasionally catch fish all day on top if there's lots of active bait, but action is most dependable when light is minimal--and you're more likely to run into calm water at these periods, too, which allows the fish to see the surface disturbance further. (Sometimes, when water is calm, lures that make minimal noise, such as the Rapala or Rebel, are highly effective, while plugs with lots of splash seem to spook the fish.)

Topwater Tuning

Topwaters are not as bulletproof as jigs or spoons--few of them last forever. The hooks, eyelets or propellers can get

26

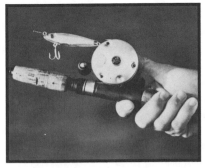

Most anglers prefer baitcasters like those from Ambassadeur or Shimano to manipulate topwaters at just the right speed. The revolving spool reels are less inclined to snarls in working the plug than are spinners.

bent by striking fish, and when this happens the action slightly changes. It may not seem like much to you, but sometimes these changes can turn a great lure into a so-so one. It's best to replace any damaged hardware, or to change lures, when a big fish bends, spindles and folds your plug. On wood or hollow plastic baits, watch for tooth penetration from trout, too--their canines can puncture the paint, cause water to infiltrate the lure body and ruin the action. If a topwater isn't highly buoyant, it's useless.

One final tip. We live in the age of catch-and-release. More minimal bag limits are being put in place every day. Topwaters carry lots of hooks, and have the potential to do a lot of harm to hooked fish, making survival after release doubtful. You can do your part for conservation by using pliers to bend down the barbs on each of your trebles before you fish the lure. It makes them far easier to remove, and that means more of the fish you put back will be there to provide sport for tomorrow.

CHAPTER 4

IN SEARCH OF MONSTER TROUT

Anybody can catch little trout. No matter where you drop your shrimp or jig in Southern inshore waters, there's always a little "speck" hanging around ready to gulp it. But catching big trout, "gators" five pounds and up, is another ball game-- one that very few anglers ever learn to play.

The big trout is a different animal from the smaller fish. His mouth (we should say "her" mouth, come to think of it, since most lunkers are female) turns bright yellow, the shoulders deepen and broaden, and food preference and habits change. While small trout survive primarily on shrimp, big ones eat mostly fish--often pretty big fish, at that. I once caught a 6-pounder that had a foot-long mullet in its gullet.

The all tackle record, 16 pounds even, came from Mason's Beach, Virginia, but big trout are far more abundant as you get further south. Of the IGFA line-class records, 11 of 15 were taken in Florida--and all but one of those on the east coast of Florida.

Big coastal rivers such as Florida's St. Johns sometimes produce large trout from deep waters, but catching the lunkers in such conditions takes most of the excitement out of it. A big trout can be a formidable adversary in shallow water, with plenty of strength to run against light gear and often some explosive, snook-like jumps to top things off.

The Indian River

There was a time when Florida's shallow Indian River, from Cocoa south, made it almost easy to land a trophy trout-- 7 pounders were common, the 10-pounder a daily possibility.

29

Biologists say that there's a separate strain of seatrout there that matures earlier and grows faster than trout anywhere else in the South. That, plus the broad, shallow flats and the abundant bait supply created perfect conditions for lots of trophy fish, and it's still probably the top spot in Florida for a fish of 5 pounds or better.

But shoreline development, gill nets and overfishing have greatly reduced the numbers of these giants of the species, to the point that a 10-pound fish is now big news there, as well as anywhere else.

Still, there are a few guys who manage to consistently find wall hangers. One of them is Jim Shupe of Winter Springs, Florida, who has one entire wall of his house papered with trout of 10 or better.

Live Bait Lunkers

Shupe's philosophy is simple. Fish where the big ones live, feed 'em what they normally eat--and be patient. He admits that he frequently spends an entire day on the water to get just one bite. But when that bite comes, it's a doozy.

For Shupe, one of the best spots for lunker trout is the Banana River, an offshoot of the Indian River, which runs into a closed section of Cape Canaveral Space Center. Shupe sees the closed area as a reservoir where trout can grow to adult size before being caught by hook and liners or scooped up in commercial nets. For years, one of Shupe's favorite areas was just outside the NASA Causeway. Now, that entire stretch of water has been closed to outboard powered boats to protect the manatees--but the closure is likely to give even further protection for big trout, and for anglers willing to pole or paddle a long way to get at them.

The bait Shupe believes in, almost exclusively, is live mullet. He likes baits six to eight inches long, far too big to be choked down by lesser trout. He castnets his own, keeping them alive in giant, aerated wells. He fishes them on light 5/0 hooks, sometimes weedless models in areas with grass or oyster shell, with stout popping rods and line testing 20 pounds to give him plenty of hook-setting authority.

He finds fish most often in water no deeper than five feet. Channel edges where tides sweep are a favorite spot, as are

Connecting with whopper trout takes patience and know-how. This big one came from Mason's Creek near Homosassa.

similar locations around shell bars. And if he gets company, Shupe moves--he believes big trout are wary and won't tolerate several boats prowling their feeding grounds.

Among the guides who specialize in fishing the Indian River area are fly-rod specialist Frank Catino and topwater expert Shawn Foster.

"There are not as many big fish as there once were," says Catino, "but in winter when they go to the canals, you can still find some very nice fish by working the docks and the mangroves over deep water. These fish are survivors because the nets can't get them under the obstructions, and not many anglers can cast accurately enough to get them, either."

Wading For Whoppers

On Florida's west coast, Richard Seward finds big trout in Tampa Bay--a location that offers tough fishing to many anglers. Seward's technique is to wade the shallows around outflows of tidal creeks, and cast to holes and cuts. Seward was once a commercial hook-and-line fishermen who perfected his techniques because he had to make a paycheck. He's now an ardent conservationist and FCA leader who releases most of his catches.

31

"A lot of the water where I catch big fish, nobody in a boat ever bothers because they think it's too shallow," he notes.

Some of this biggest trout have come from water only 2 feet deep--water where he switches to braided Dacron line, because it has more buoyancy than monofilament and doesn't sink into grass or shell. He adds a 3-foot leader of clear mono to cut visibility at the lure.

Seward says wading is the only way to fish these shallows, because boats nearly always spook the fish. He relies on artificials--his lure box contains plastic-tailed jigs, slow sinking plugs such as the 52-M MirrOlure, and a selection of noisy topwaters including the Bill Norman Rat-Lure.

Fishing is usually best in his waters during the cooler months, when fish move onto the flats on temperate days, schooling into the channels on cold nights.

"Look for moving water," Seward suggests. "It can be coming in or going out, but unless it's moving the big ones won't feed."

One of his favorite techniques for a lunker is to cast a jig up-tide along the edge of an oyster bar and let the current sweep it back down, tumbling along bottom.

"They lay right at the drop, waiting for bait to come down where they can trap it against the edge," he notes. "The biggest fish usually take these preferred feeding stations."

Offshore Combos

Further north along the Gulf Coast, Steve Marusak of New Port Richey--inventor of the Cotee Jig--has made a reputation for catching big trout throughout the hottest days of summer.

He does so by fishing the broad grass flats 5 to 14 feet deep from Tarpon Springs northward--flats that extend up to five miles offshore in some areas.

"There's endless habitat in an area like this, and there are bound to be quite a few big trout there all the time," he notes. "But the big ones stay buried in the grass during the day. Unless you put a bait right down in there with them, they won't touch it."

Marusak scores on big fish by casting his jigs ahead of a drifting boat, letting them sink all the way into the grass, and

Big trout love oyster bars. The largest trout, biologists say, tend to be loners, and all the larger fish are females.

then barely crawling them along through the weeds. He's developed a fine sense of touch that helps him distinguish the difference between the mouthing of a big trout and the pull of a weed, and he consistently lands fish in the five-pound class-- as well as hundreds of smaller ones.

Marusak makes weedless jigs, and uses them when weeds are especially thick. Favorite colors in lure tails are rootbeer and lime green. He fishes heads weighing anywhere from 1/8 to 3/8 ounces, depending on the speed of the drift.

"You need enough weight to get the bait down there before you drift over it," he notes, "but in general, the lighter the head, the more strikes you get."

He fishes the lures on graphite spinning rods--a must, he says, to help distinguish strikes from weeds--with 8- to 10-pound test line.

Marusak also likes to change techniques in winter, when unusual numbers of lunker trout school around powerplant outlets in the area. Guide Everett Antrim, known as "Mr. Trout" to anyone who has fished with him, showed Marusak the tricks of working the power plants.

"A day or two after the first big winter front arrives, with freezing temperatures, I'll be at the Crystal River Powerplant," he says. "The concentration of really big fish in that area and other hotwater outflows can be amazing." (Florida's only west coast IGFA line class record came from this area--a 12-pound, 8 ounce monster taken in 1983.)

In the deep water and sometimes swift current of these areas, he often switches to heavier jigs, and also to night fishing--though the cold makes it tough. But Marusak figures it's worth paying your dues to tangle with the whoppers.

Fighting Big Trout

David Fairbanks, now with Coastal Lures and formerly of MirrOlure, is a noted expert on handling giant trout and other inshore species on light lines, having held five IGFA records in the 2-pound and 4-pound class. He says the tricks of using spider-web line can be applied effectively with more conventional tackle.

"One of the things I learned is that the less pressure you put on trout, the fewer you lose," he notes. "With small fish you can reel them right to the boat and jerk them in like a tournament bass fisherman, but you try that with a fish over 5 pounds and you'll lose her almost every time."

Fairbanks advises setting the hook lightly, even with heavy line, because of the soft mouths of the trout. It's then a matter of gently guiding the fish toward the boat, dropping the rod tip to ease the drag when she runs, raising it to gain line when she turns toward you. He keeps his rod tip low to discourage the fish from wallowing on top or jumping, which he says often allows them to throw the plug.

And he never hurries a fish at boatside, allowing it to run off repeatedly if it has the power, until finally the landing net can be slid underneath for the final scoop.

To Net Or Not

"You never know where the hook is until you have the fish in your hands," he says. "If you play each one like it's barely hooked, you'll rarely lose one."

Fairbanks advocates using a net on all trout over 2 pounds, even if you're fishing stout line. Many fish are lost when an angler tries to derrick them over the side.

But, if you're fishing a treble-hooked plug, netting every fish means you spend more time untangling plug and fish than you do casting.

Big trout don't discriminate against little fishermen. This 7-pounder came from the Banana River and was caught on a live shrimp fished near a spoil bar at dawn.

Karl Wickstrom, publisher of Florida Sportsman Magazine and a devout trout angler, suggests simply "guarding" all but the largest fish with the net--when the fish is worn out, you slip the net below it and then hoist the fish into the boat via rod and line, but keep the net about half-way up its body without ever actually scooping the fish inside. The net mesh never gets up to where the hooks are, so can't tangle--yet, if the fish flops off, she drops into the net.

It also helps to use the rubber-mesh "tangle-free" nets, rather than conventional nylon. The rubber mesh is not as strong as nylon and sun ruins it in a couple of years, but it's definitely much better about releasing your hooks.

Of course, in these conservation conscious days, you may not want to net your fish at all, since the nets rub off the slime coat and make the fish more susceptible to disease. If you plan to release your catch anyway, it's probably best to avoid the net--but if it's a wall-hanger, scoop away.

Flyrodding For Gators

Big trout can also be caught on flyrod poppers with some regularity. Bullet-head "sliders" about three inches long are the ticket, with sparse feather or Mylar dressing. Soft foam bugs are the hot item these days among inshore saltwater flyrodders, and these can be either shaped as popper or slider heads. Trout seem to hang on to them after the take, which gives a better chance to set the hook. Also good are hair bugs like those in the Dahlberg system and those designed by Jim Stewart of Tampa for Umpqua. Again, the soft bodies inspire trout to eat them instead of spit them out.

The Deceiver in Cockroach color is a good shrimp imitation among streamers. Also, small glass minnow patterns work well when trout are in the creeks in late fall and early winter.

Rods in the 8- to 9-weight class are the ticket for trout, with my personal favorite presently a little Orvis HLS 8-weight, 9-foot graphite that comes in four pieces. The thing can be stuck under the boat seat, completely out of the way, until you get a yen to flex the long rod.

The middle-weight gear makes for easy casting of typical trout-sized flies and bugs, and provides for a spectacular fight when one is hooked. Fly-rod gear is particularly effective when fish gather along mangrove shorelines or under docks, because you can splat the bug in there on a fixed line length every time, yet pick it up quickly and not waste time retrieving through barren water.

CHAPTER 5

IT'S THE REAL THING

It's almost cheating.

At times, they can't seem to resist. Live bait may make it too easy to catch trout.

Except when it doesn't.

There's no question that most of the time, trout become suckers and flounder all over themselves when a live shrimp comes drifting by overhead, yet won't touch a plug or jig. It's no fluke, but--hey, why carp about it?

If you can't lick 'em, join 'em. (Just don't try any fish-name jokes at the bait shop.)

Trout are particularly susceptible to live baits, I suspect, because they are fairly deliberate fish, often given to a close inspection of their food--sort of the way a suspicious 8-year-old pushes a piece of meat around on his plate, flips it over to study the underside--you know. This sometimes keeps trout from eating artificials, and also keeps kids from eating liver, no matter how many times Mom tells them it's steak.

There are times when live bait will outfish lures 10 to 1. There are also times when lures will outfish livebaits. But there will never be a time when kids will eat liver. (Me either.)

Shrimp For Trout

There's no question that shrimp is the feeler's up favorite for sea trout, probably accounting for far more "specks" each year than all other baits combined.

Shrimp are easy to buy, easy to keep alive in a couple gallons of cool saltwater, and easy to fish. But there's more to it than impaling one on a 5/0 and anchoring it in a channel with an ounce of lead.

Trout most often take shrimp that are swimming around up in the water column, and that's where your bait should be. Thus, shrimp generally do best with little or no weight, and that includes minimal weight from the hook.

You'll catch a lot more fish on a size 2 to size 6 light wire, of the type used by freshwater crappie fishermen, than you will using bigger "ocean" sized (/0) models. The thin wire weighs much less than the heavier stuff, so the shrimp can swim more easily, and the thin diameter is less likely to kill the bait when it is put in place.

And, since livebaiting for trout pretty much requires light gear of 8-pound-test or less, there's little danger of straightening the light hook, provided your drag is set properly to protect that light line. (Remember, the safe setting is about 1/3 the rated strength--which is to say under 3 pounds for 8-pound test.)

There are a couple of proven hook-ups for shrimp that keep the bait alive and swimming. The most common is just under the crest or horn on the head, just behind the eyes. The hook can be slid in here, just penetrating the shell on both sides, with minimal damage. Don't sink it down into the center of the head area, because the shrimp's carburetor and fuel pump are in there, and it will break down immediately if any of that stuff is touched.

Properly hooked this way, the shrimp can swim freely, and can even come to the surface and hop around when it gets the inclination. (When it does that, hang on to your rod.)

The second rig is through the last joint of the tail, again running the hook sideways so it doesn't hit the nerve chord. The tail fin is usually cut off on this rig, which naturally enough makes it tough for the shrimp to swim, but if you need maximum distance, this hook-up will stand the necessary casting force better. It also works well in murky water, because the broken tail joint puts out shrimp smell that trout can home in on.

There are also shrimp harnesses, like those put out by Pico, which snuggle the shrimp into a spring-loaded device that grips it without actually penetrating the shell. These are

Live shrimp are easy to get and deadly for trout in most areas most of the year. It's a good idea to fish them on a small hook as shown here, so that they stay alive and swim naturally.

especially good for drifting or slow-trolling a shrimp, because most will keep the shrimp in the upright swimming position.

In general, big shrimp (if you'll permit us the oxymoron) swim a lot better than small shrimp when they're toting a hook. So when you can, opt for "select" or "jumbo" shrimp, even though they're more expensive. You'll catch more trout and bigger ones for the extra investment--unless, of course, there are pinfish or ladyfish around. (If the fish don't bite, the jumbos do better on a shish-ka-bob, too.)

Sardines

In areas where scaled sardines and threadfin herring are found, these flat-sided, silvery fish make wonderful bait, particularly for larger trout. They're extremely active on the hook and can be seen for long distances because of their flashing sides, so they combine the action of an artificial with the scent and sonic attraction of the real thing.

Scaled sardines or "whitebait" can be chummed in on grass flats from 3 to 5 feet deep with a mix of canned jack mackerel and whole wheat bread, and then cast-netted. Threadfins, also known as "greenbacks", don't come to the chum, but can often be netted along the beaches by watching for the "shad ripple" they make as they feed at the surface.

Both species are very delicate and require a large, flow-through baitwell for survival, though you can keep a half-dozen at a time in a baitbucket suspended in a flowing tide.

There are a number of hook-ups for these baits, with the most common being through the nose just ahead of the eyes. This is relatively tough and the baits won't spin in a strong tide. Also effective is hooking just ahead of the ventral fin, which makes for more dart and flash, but the bait will spin in strong flows. Hooking right behind the dorsal also is effective, particularly if you're trying to swim them up under mangroves or docks, because you can sometimes "steer" them with slight pressure on the line with this rigging.

Sardines definitely attract big trout, as well as jumbo reds, snook, tarpon and whatever else might be on the flats. So some anglers fish them on somewhat heavier hooks, 1/0 or 2/0 livebait hooks with short shanks, and line testing up to 12 pounds or so. A couple feet of 30-pound shock leader will prevent cut-offs if a snook grabs the bait.

Mullet

Finger mullet--and sometimes much larger sizes--are very attractive to big trout. They're particularly good on the Atlantic Coast during the spring and fall migrations, when thousands of the 4- to 6-inch long baitfish pour into the lagoons and bays.

Trout--and everything else that swims--gorge themselves on the baits, which are easily caught by castnet on the shallow flats, passes or the ocean surf

The baits can be rigged and fished much like the sardines indicated above, but they're bigger, heavier and somewhat more durable. They also tend to catch bigger trout, though you may have to wait a long time for a fish big enough to eat your bait to come by if you hang an 8-incher out there.

Lively Live Bait Action

Though you can catch some fish on live bait by simply hanging one out there in the current, it works a lot better if you apply yourself a bit. For one thing, most strikes come when the live bait approaches the fish naturally, with the current. This means that unless you're drifting in a boat, you

Scaled sardines, also known as "whitebait", are a favorite along much of the Gulf Coast. They're effective for big trout, as well as for snook, reds and other species.

have to make a lot of casts to keep the presentation looking right.

The trick is to cast either from below or to the side of the area you want to fish, so that the tide sweeps it over the fish. As soon as it drifts past the likely contact point, you reel in and present it again, a few feet farther on. It's a good bit of work and it does in the bait in four or five throws, but you catch a lot more fish than with a static presentation most of the time.

You can also greatly improve your catch at times by chumming with the live bait. Tossing a few free shrimp (use the little ones for this) or some extra sardines into a hole or around a creekmouth will definitely turn on fish that may be lazing there, so that when the one with the hook in it arrives, they're thinking about chow time.

41

Pop Them Up

The popping cork is a deadly device for keeping live bait suspended at trout depth, and trout are particularly susceptible to the "BALOOP" that a cork makes when it's jerked under water. The sound is a lot like that made by a trout hitting on top, and it often attracts them from considerable distances to get in on the feed.

The mistake some make is popping the cork too often. About once a minute is maximum, and better is every two or three minutes. In between, either let the rig drift with the tide or just slowly retrieve the thing, at less than walking pace, so that the bait swims around naturally.

It's not a bad idea, when fishing light line, to run about four feet of 20-pound-test leader to the hook. Crimp the cork on the upper end of this leader, rather than on your lighter running line. That way, the running line is less likely to be weakened.

There are times when the no-lead advice given earlier has to be broken, of course. When you find trout feeding in deep grass, 8 to 10 feet down, you have to add a quarter-ounce rubber core or similar weight to get the bait down where they'll see it. Ditto when they're in the deep holes in winter. But even then, keep the weight as light as possible to reach bottom, and keep the bait moving--you'll catch more trout.

Glass Minnows

The annual glass minnow invasion of coastal rivers begins in early November most years on Florida's Gulf Coast, and is on at full bore from Thanksgiving to Christmas from the Anclote River southward. Anglers who know the tricks of fishing this migration load their boats with trout, as well as a mix of snook, reds and countless ladyfish and jacks.

The minute minnows, thought to be anchovy or sardine spawn by many local guides, are only a half-inch long, but they come into the rivers with the cooling temperatures in countless millions, filling the rivers from shore to shore with black, swarming masses.

This sort of food supply never goes unnoticed in Nature, and the fish follow. (They're following their own natural

Sardines are best caught with a large castnet, as manned here by Terra Ceia guide James Wood. The baits are chummed into range with a mix of whole wheat bread, canned mackerel and canned sardines.

migration, as well, as they move toward the deep holes where they'll spend the cold snaps of winter.)

Though it's hard to imagine that large fish would pay much attention to bait that is hardly bigger than a thumbtack, most inshore gamefish stuff themselves with the minnows for as long as they are available.

Even whopper snook can be seen charging through the schools of tiny baits, often with their backs out of water as they crash and churn the surface. And when a school of ladyfish goes on a feed in the minnows, they can turn an acre or more of water into white foam.

Fishing can be ridiculously easy if you get on the areas where the minnows are most dense.

The only stickler is that this is one live bait that's too small to catch in a conventional bait net, and if you could catch them they're too small to stay alive on the hook. So this is one "live bait" run that you fish with artificials--tiny silver-tailed jigs, spoons no more than 2 inches long, and epoxy or Mylar silver streamer flies.

Finding the right spot in the river sometimes takes some study. The glass minnows seem to gather in certain areas in great numbers, and are completely absent in others. If you fish where the minnows are missing, you won't catch much, because every fish in the river is likely to be homed in on them at this time of year.

The most obvious way to spot the bait, of course, is to luck up on a feeding frenzy--trout, ladyfish, jacks, and snook all busting bait on top. This is most likely on the first part of the rising tide, especially if this comes at dawn or dusk.

If you're not lucky enough to see a school of fish breaking, sometimes the concentrations are given away by a few scattered splashes, particularly on flats adjacent to deeper pools in the river, where they'll push the bait to attack.

Concentrations of diving pelicans are also a good indicator of minnows in the river. There's not much else to draw pelicans inland, so when you see them crashing well upstream, you can bet the glass minnows are there.

Wading birds also work hard on the minnows, so you might fish in areas where you see a number of egrets or herons.

West coast rivers that frequently produce glass minnow action in fall include the Anclote, Pithlachascotee, Palm, Alafia, Little Manatee, Manatee, Myakka and Peace. Fishing usually remains good at least through the first frost of winter.

CHAPTER 6

GETTING THE DRIFT

Do you know how to "drive" your boat with the engine shut off? Most anglers don't pay much attention to boat control once they turn off the ignition, but knowing how to manage a drift is one of the keys to successful fishing for a wide variety of species including not only seatrout but also redfish and snook inshore, bonefish, permit and tarpon on the Florida flats and cobia on the outside buoys.

The better you can steer without power, and the less often you have to start that big, noisy outboard, the more fish you'll catch as a general rule.

Steering Without Power

So how can you "steer" without the motor running? The most basic technique is to use your outboard's lower unit as a rudder, just like the rudder on a sailboat. It works remarkably well. An outboard with the motor in the full "down" position always drifts with the transom to the wind because of the drag of the prop. Since the wind-power is being applied from the usual direction aft, you can readily steer the boat by simply turning the wheel in the direction you want to go, at angles up to about 45 degrees from straight ahead.

After that, the wind striking the side of the boat will force it back to a more nearly straight direction, but the latitude allowed is often enough to enable you to make a perfect drift along the edge of a grass line, oyster bar or mangrove shoreline without ever starting the engine, touching a push pole or turning on a trolling motor.

Slowing The Drift

Okay, but suppose you're drifting too fast? No problem. Take the anchor off the chain (yes, you should definitely have 6 to 10 feet of chain on your anchor, even for an inshore boat) and trail chain and line aft. The chain won't snag as the anchor would, but it will create enough drag that your drift will slow considerably.

Or, in deep water, you can get the same result by trailing a five-gallon bucket on a yoke line from the stern cleats. The bucket creates considerable drag, greatly cutting down boat speed. There are also commercial "sea anchors" made of metal rods and canvas that accomplish the same thing.

If you use a stern-mount electric trolling motor on your boat, you can also slow the boat, and do some steering, by setting the motor in reverse on its lowest speed.

Getting Sideways

If you're fishing with several companions, you may want to drift a flat sideways, so that everybody has equal access to the fish. To make that happen, you simply move the chain and line or sea anchor forward to create drag there. This drag can be adjusted by letting out more line to increase it or pulling in until the chain is partly out of water to reduce it, until it exactly counterbalances the drag of the outboard astern, and presto, you're floating sideways. (Be sure to assign one man to get this line aboard if you hook a big fish, however--it represents a nasty obstacle otherwise.)

If you run a bow mount trolling motor on your boat, you can get the same result by lowering that motor as a counter to the outboard. On most boats, the drag of the troller's prop and lower unit is adequate to turn the boat broadside to the wind. To steer, you apply an occasional burst of power via the electric.

When you're drifting this way, you'll catch most of your fish by casting downwind, of course--but it often pays to hang a lightweight jig with a swimmer tail off the upwind side of the boat as well. Adjust the line length so that it skims along just off bottom, letting out more line in deeper areas or for a fast drift, less for shallow water or slowing drift. The fish tend to

A trolling motor can help maintain the drift that puts you on trout when drifting an open bay. Avoid using your outboard, because its noise can end a bite in a hurry.

follow the lure for a long way before making up their mind, and this gives them lots of opportunity to take.

Sailing The Flats

There will be times, on nearly windless days in summer, when you'll find you're actually drifting too slow to cover the water and find fish. When that happens, you can speed the drift a bit by creating more "sail" area. Put up your Bimini, and you'll be surprised at how this oddly shaped canvas wing catches the wind and increases your motion. Your angling partners will appreciate the shade, too, though they may not appreciate the way the top gets in the way of backcasts.

When the water is rough, you may find it safest to drift with the bow into the wind, thus keeping the slop from coming in over the low transom. To do that, you trail chain and line or bucket and line from the bow cleat and trim the motor up out of the water.

47

By lowering the outboard while drifting, you can assure that the boat will drift with the bow downwind. You can then steer the boat to some degree by turning the wheel, using the skeg as a rudder.

You can't do much steering when you drift this way, but sometimes it's the only way to keep water out of the cockpit. (The five-gallon bucket works OK for boats up to about 20 feet in moderate winds. With larger boats and stronger winds, you need a regular drogue or sea anchor. The larger models of these will really slow you down, and can also be used in emergencies if your outboard breaks down offshore and you must keep the bow into the wind to stay afloat.)

Putting On The Brakes

When you drift shallow bays for trout, it's essential to stop the boat immediately when you find action. Otherwise, you drift right down on top of the school and blow them out of the location.

To be ready to stop the boat quickly, you need a heavy anchor, on deck and ready to drop immediately when somebody hooks up with a fish.

Many anglers try to save a few bucks by buying a lightweight anchor, but these don't do the job. It's always wise to buy an anchor designed for a larger boat, rather than the "right" size, because the bigger one--while it may cost you an extra $15 to $20--will actually ANCHOR you, in all conditions, and do it

Drifting while you cast ahead of the boat with slow-sinking plugs or jigs is an easy, effective way to find schools of trout in waters you don't know well.

quickly. A length of heavy, galvanized chain, as mentioned above, will keep the shaft down and help the anchor dig in quickly.

Light patent anchors like the Danforth will do the job, too, but you have to let out a lot of line to get them to stick if there's any wind or current at all. It always takes a length of line three times the water depth to make an anchor hold, and often takes five to seven times the depth. And if you let out a hundred feet of rode and the trout are a hundred feet downwind, you wind up right on top of them. This is no problem if you're fishing in 20 feet of murky water in Lake Pontchartrain, but it's a big problem if you're drifting 8 feet of glass-clear flats off Homosassa--the trout leave long before the boat gets stopped. A big, heavy anchor stops you when you need to stop, pronto.

Getting control of your drift not only lets you cover the water better, but the fact that you start the engine less frequently means you scare fewer fish. In these days of lots of boats, diminished habitat and lower limits, that can be a major factor in a successful day on the water.

49

CHAPTER 7

JIGS AND SPOONS

Remember when the Trout Tout arrived on the scene? Suddenly, speckled trout catches went through the ceiling, because everybody became an artificial lure expert overnight. The "artificial shrimp" has spread to dozens of companies and appears in hundreds of shapes, but it's still just as effective now as it was when it first hit the water 25 years ago. Jigs sell big because they work.

Soft Plastics

The big advantage of soft plastics like those made by Cotee, 12-Fathom, Culprit, Bubba, Mann's, Berkley and many others is that they are chewable. When a trout takes hold, he tries to swallow the lure instead of spitting it out. This makes it far easier for the average angler to realize that a.) I've got a bite, and b.) I should think about setting the hook. It has been the demise of probably more trout than have been scooped up by all the gillnet boats at work in the last two decades, though God knows the net boys have worked hard at adding up the numbers.

Plastic jig tails come in many shapes besides the basic shrimp, and most of them work. My personal favorite is the "shad tail", which has a bulbous tail that wiggles madly when the lure is drawn through the water. Curly-tail swimmers are also very good, and of course some experts like Steve Marusak of Cotee and guide Everett Antrim, known as "Mr. Trout", prefer the straight paddle-tail version.

51

Also very effective of late has been a plastic shrimp with a separate double hook that hides inside the body, produced by D.O.A. Lures. The bait comes through the water exactly like a swimming shrimp, and it can be deadly for those with the patience to fish it slowly.

Plastic-tailed jigs usually are most effective for trout when allowed to sink near bottom, then worked with slight twitches of the rod tip. The lure should move quickly, but not far-- maybe only 3 or 4 inches. You don't want the big, yard-long hops that work so well for Spanish mackerel, just little jumps that keep the lure off bottom.

Adjust the head weight to the depth of the water, so that the bait stays within a foot of bottom at your favored retrieve speed. And stay alert--a take often feels like a bit of weed, or sometimes there's only a slight tick on the line. In either case, promptly set the hook.

Any color is OK so long as it's gold flake.

No, actually, any color you like is probably OK with the trout. In general, go with light, silvery colors in clear water, dark colors in dark water. Chartreuse is a popular shade, as is rootbeer and smoke and a bunch of others.

Return Of The Bucktail

Old lures never die, but many are consigned to forgotten corners of the tacklebox over the years. One is the hair jig, once one of the most popular of all artificials, now rarely seen either on the water or in a tackle shop.

Hair jigs, most commonly tied with bucktail but also popularly dressed with nylon in later years, were displaced almost overnight by the phenomenal rise of soft plastic jig bodies about 20 years ago. End of hair jigs, as far as most anglers were concerned.

But Vance Tice, who started out a few years ago with his soft plastic "Bubba Jigs", says he thinks anglers gave up on hair jigs too soon, and he has introduced an entire series to his line.

Jigs made from hair or filament have some advantages that soft plastics don't, Tice says, and they're particularly useful in the cooler months of the year when most fish go deep in the

52

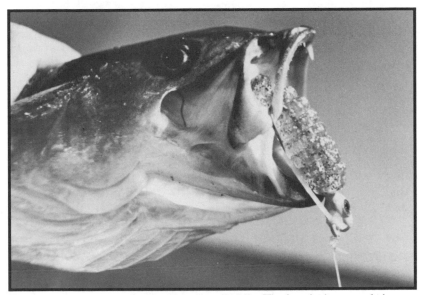

Trout can't seem to resist the plastic-tailed jig. The lure imitates a shrimp or a small minnow, both favored trout foods.

ship channels and turning basins and settle into holes in coastal rivers.

Jigs made of natural hair, including bucktail and calftail, have a buoyancy that keeps them in the water column for a long, slow, fluttering drop. When the fish are cold and slow, that's exactly the sort of presentation that makes them eat.

When fished slowly on the bottom, a hair jig will "breathe" even as it sits still, the hair pulsing in the current. When fish like seatrout are lethargic, they often ignore everything else, but will scoop up a bucktail off bottom. (Some hair jigs have a bit of maribou feather tied in, and this extremely soft material waves and dances wildly in the slightest current.)

Tice says that hair jigs are also far more durable than most plastic-tailed jigs. A single hair jig will usually last all day, while soft plastics often require a dozen or more tails in a good day when lots of fish are caught.

For anglers who like to use liquid scent such as Fish Formula or menhaden oil on their lures, the hair jig soaks up the scent and holds it for many casts while plastic baits need doped after each cast.

Fishing bucktails in winter takes a bit of patience. It requires a considerable time for the 1/8 to 1/4 ounce sizes to hit bottom, and once they do the best retrieve is often hardly a retrieve at all. The lure is twitched and crawled more than hopped, because each twitch brings the hair alive. There's plenty of action, without much speed--and that's the sort of retrieve that does the job when the fish are cold.

When a fish takes, often there's only a slight tap on the line. You have to be ready for it and set the hook quickly. Most fish don't go ahead and swallow the bucktail as they will a soft plastic.

To be sure, hair jigs are not about to displace soft plastics. They don't cast as far because of their bulk, and fish don't hang on to them the way they do soft, molded bodies. They can't be molded into the precise shapes that plastics can, and if you want to change the size or color of the lure, you have to cut one off and tie on another, rather than simply replacing the tail as with plastics.

Finally, they hold saltwater, and have to be rinsed in fresh at the end of each trip, or they tend to carry salt into the tackle box, not only rusting the jig hook but anything nearby as well.

But they are a useful tool, in the right place and at the right time, and probably ought to be a part of the arsenal of the complete angler once again.

The Spoon

While trout often take weedless redfish spoons, they're not the best choice for them. For reasons known only to themselves, trout much prefer more conventional spoon designs such as the Johnson Sprite, the Cotee Live-Eye, Accetta Pet, Krockodile and Kastmaster. These are basic, teardrop spoons that come from the factory with small treble hooks attached with a ring eye.

They're light in weight and have a wider wobble than weedless spoons, and the Sprite has a tiny red tag of plastic on the split ring that seems to bring extra strikes, just as do the decal "eyes" on the Cotee until they wear off, and the red feather on the Pet.

Bucktails work well because they sink slowly and have a lifelike action even at moderate retrieve speeds.

Sometimes the fish prefer silver, sometimes gold, and one day the tiny 1/6 ounce model does the job while the next they want a bigger mouthful. It's smart to go prepared with a selection. But whichever you fish, it should be tied direct to about 18 inches of shock leader--20-pound-test mono--which is then fastened to the running line with a very small barrel swivel.

The swivel is a must, because all spoons twist line a bit, even though they wobble instead of spin most of the time. If you don't use the swivel, particularly with spinning gear, you'll spend half the day pulling bird's nest from your line. However, don't make the beginner's mistake of attaching a snap and swivel direct to the spoon--this interferes with the action, and the extra hardware seems to reduce the number of strikes some days.

Finally, in these days of catch-and-release fishing, it makes sense to flatten the barbs of the hooks before you make your first cast. This makes it far easier to release a trout alive, and you'll rarely lose a fish because of it.

Trout are generally less likely to "freight train" a lure than are reds. They like to swim up, look it over, and then decide whether to hit, which means that a lure that hesitates every now and then is more appealing to them. They prefer smaller

Spoons have a fatal attraction for trout, even though they're not particularly popular among trout anglers in many areas.

sizes, too--even though they'll readily attack a 5-inch topwater, in spoons they seem to prefer nothing longer than 2 1/2 inches.

Spoon Dancing

These lures all have to be "danced" through the water to gain maximum efficiency on trout--the straight, steady retrieve that works so well on reds is not as effective here. Fishing over grass in two to six feet of water spring through fall, the routine is to let them sink a foot or so, then begin a slow retrieve as you wiggle and shake the rod tip steadily. The spoon goes into a sort of St. Vitus dance, rising, sinking, hesitating and flashing as it comes back toward the boat. The impression, probably, is of a wounded sardine or pinfish trying to regain equilibrium. Whatever, the trout can't stand it.

You'll get a lot of hits that don't connect with the hooks, because the lure is frequently falling on a slack line when the strike comes. But the spoon seems to make trout crazy enough that they'll usually keep coming back for another try until you sink the barbs.

Big trout are partial to a darting spoon. A simple cast-and-retrieve works, but a dancing, hesitating action does much better.

Winter Spoon Jigging

Spoons can also be effective as jigging lures in the dead of winter, when trout, reds and other species gang up in dredge holes, shipping ports and deeper coastal rivers. Here, you want lots of weight and no planing surfaces--chromed lead or cast spoons like the Hopkins Shorty are the ticket. They're basically just a thick, straight chunk of metal. The way you fish them is to graph water 20 feet or deeper until you find a school of inverted V's.

Inverted V's eat spoons.

So drop the spoon straight down next to the gunnel, and then yo-yo the lure up and down with sharp flicks of the rod tip, allowing it to fall on an almost-but-not-quite-slack line as you lower the rod tip. The lure darts toward the surface three or four feet, then flutters back. Hits invariably come on the fall. All you feel is a slight tick or bump on the line. In order to translate that into a fish, you have to set the hook instantly.

I've caught trout, reds, blues, jacks, ladyfish, mangrove snapper, drum, sea bass and a little bit of everything else with this technique. It doesn't work all the time, but when you pass over a hole and see a pile of fish marking on the recorder, it will do the job.

57

Trolling Spoons

While it's no big secret that you can catch offshore fish by trolling spoons, not many folks try it inshore. There used to be a group of old-timers who wore out the trout, snook and reds in the 10,000 Islands area of Florida by towing spoons close to the mangroves and oyster bars, but the practice died out two decade ago. It still works, I can report from personal experience, and can be a good way to find fish on those days when they seem to have disappeared. Pull till you get a hook-up, then stop and work the area over with jigs and live bait.

Whatever the spoon you use or the fish you're after, you can always make the lure more effective by adding a small strip of porkrind to the hook to give it a bit of extra wiggle. Don't go for big chunks or for extra long strips, because they tend to interfere with the normal action of the spoon, but the smaller strips, usually called "spinning" size, really do make an already great lure even better.

CHAPTER 8

IT'S HOT WHEN IT'S COLD-- WINTER TROUT

The old man appeared to be asleep.

His hat drooped down over his face. Goofy hat, one of those Russian jobs with ear flaps. His head nodded, shoulders slumped, and he leaned forward with each exhalation, so much that I was concerned he'd fall out of the boat, or at the very least drop his rod overboard. You couldn't blame him for nodding off--the morning sun had burned off the January chill, and I was feeling drowsy myself.

But every time the old guy breathed in and leaned back, he gave that rod one slow, upward twitch.

About the tenth time he did it, the rod tip went down, the old man quit playing possum, and a big, yellow-mouthed trout came flopping to the surface of the Salt River.

He sat there and caught eight more while my partner and I, and a lot of other people close by, flailed the hole to a froth with our more vigorous presentations, to no avail.

To add insult to injury, he actually did go to sleep when the fish quit biting. So we did the only honorable thing. We ran the trolling motor over next to him and looked inside his boat to see what he was using.

He had two extra rods in there, and both of them wore little bitty yellow jigs, about the size you'd use for crappie fishing. There were half-a-dozen more jigs and plastic tails scattered on the boat seat. My partner wanted to reach in there and snitch one, but I opined that spying was enough.

We switched to the jigs we had, whaled away, and still didn't catch anything. Even though, I blush to admit, we cast right into the spot in front of the sleeping angler.

Problem was, I later figured out, that we didn't think like Eskimos.

To you and me, snow is snow, right? But to an Eskimo, there are 37 or 50 or a hundred and some kinds of snow, it says in National Geographic.

Same with winter trout lures. There's no such thing as a generic when it comes to piquing the testy appetites of winter trout. They can be very particular in what they want in terms of weight, size, color and presentation, and you might have to understand and sort through a lot of variations in order to come up with the right combination.

Slower And Deeper

The first thing to learn, say many experts, is that if you aren't catching winter fish, you need to go deeper and slower. When the big cold fronts arrive, the Big Three of the flats, along with just about everything else in inshore coastal areas crowd into the deep holes, turning basins, dredged canals, spring-fed rivers and powerplant outfalls, trying to avoid the chill on the flats. They're lethargic, and they want as much insulating water above them as possible, so they settle into the deepest water they can find in these areas.

The jig is an excellent tool for excavating them from these spots, to be sure. But it has a few problems.

For one thing, a heavy jig does not know when to quit sinking. It will plummet right on down past the fish and latch on to bottom if you're not careful. (For some reason, all the good holes have gnarly, snaggery, snatchery bottoms that positively gobble up tackle!) And, on the other hand, if you keep it moving fast enough to avoid the snags, you may also keep it moving fast enough to avoid those somnambulistic lunker trout and reds.

Go Light

One of the tricks of retaining your tackle, and your sanity, is to fish jigs with lighter heads than those normally used on the coast, but to rig them with tails as large or larger than the

A jig worked slow and deep did the job on this winter trout taken in Bull Bay by the author's son with guide Larry Mendez. Winter trout concentrations are a good place to get young anglers started.

norm. The common jig sizes for inshore fish are 1/4 and 3/8-ounce heads, and those will catch fish much of the time. But when they're making it tough, a switch down to a 1/8-ounce head is often magic.

You go to a smaller head, but not a smaller tail. The combination of the light head and the fairly buoyant and bulky tail results in a slow, fluttering drop into the depths, and that's often just what you need to turn on fish enduring the Big Chill.

And, while the stout hooks of the typical saltwater jig are just the thing in heavier lures, for winter fishing with a light bait, you might want to try something with a light wire hook like those used on freshwater walleye and crappie jigs.

Reason?

First, because you can actually keep such a jig on the end of your line, instead of delivering it in a single cast to add to the tons of jettisoned jigs that line the bottom of most good winter holes. The light wire hook can be sprung or straightened when you snag, so you get it back, if you use reasonably heavy line--and this can be as light as 8-pound-test with some jigs.

Secondly, those fine wire hooks penetrate very quickly, and often hook the fish without any help on your part--very important in catching winter trout, because often the bite is only the slightest tick on the line, not enough to tip you off if you're not setting on ready. But with the fine wire hooks, the

61

Spinning gear with a light but stiff graphite rod makes it possible to maintain contact with jigs and slow-sinking plugs despite the slow retrieve speed.

trout often snags itself as it turns away with the jig in its mouth, even if you don't do anything but hold tension.

The standard grub tail catches plenty of winter trout, but the swimmer tails are often a bit better. They sink slower because of that wiggling tail, creating more drag on the drop, and they give the lure more action without more speed through the water. The thing looks alive even when it's pretty much idling along, and that can be a big advantage when fish are too cold to move very much.

Slow-sinking plugs also do very well in winter, and once you get the timing down, you can suspend them just off bottom. They work at least as well as jigs, though some take more patience because they sink TOO slowly. The trick is to carry a selection and match the density to the water depth.

Action—But Not Much

The best action for winter fish varies. On extremely cold days, the very slow rise and fall demonstrated by the old gentleman on the Salt River can be effective.

More commonly, a fairly steady series of small hops, just barely clearing the bottom, will do the job. The idea is to convince the fish that it's alive, but not to swim it out of their strike range, which can be very limited in cold water.

Tandem jig rigs like these from Love Lures often result in doubleheaders. The two light lures provide casting weight and a slow drop.

The rod tip should move only a few inches to impart action--the sharp, lengthy whips that work well in spring and summer are not the ticket in winter.

The take is often light, perhaps just a tap, or you may feel nothing, but see the line jump. If you have any suspicions, set the hook quickly, with a short, upward flip of the rod tip. No need to "cross his eyes" as they do in catching largemouths on a plastic worm--trout have soft mouths, and a hard set not only is unnecessary, but can actually jerk the hook right through the flesh so that the fish escapes.

Dualies

One of the problems with tossing light jigs is that you can't toss them very far, especially if you use anything other than very light spinning tackle and spider-webby mono, and if you use that stuff you lose most of your jigs on bottom.

Catch 22?

Not necessarily. If you want to fish jigs on heavier spinning gear or on baitcasters, you can add a second jig and still enjoy most of the benefits of a single, plus some extras.

Using two very light jigs, 1/8 ounce or less, gives you adequate weight for casting, but since neither lure is very heavy and since they have a stout leader suspended between them creating lots of drag, they sink slowly--just what you want for winter fishing.

Plus, the two jigs going through the water sometimes seem to better catch the attention of the fish than a single.

And the best part--when you hook one, you often get a second as it rushes in to take the gyrating jig that is following the hooked fish. It happens regularly when you find a good school of trout.

The best dual rigs are imitations of those perfected by the Love Lure Company in St. Petersburg, Florida. A pair of 1/8 or 1/16 ounce heads are connected by a length of 20-pound-test mono, which has a simple loop knot about two thirds of the way up its 3-foot length. This causes one jig to hang about a foot from the end of the running line, the other to hang about 2 feet from the end. Love uses a small barrel swivel in the loop to provide a convenient tie for the running line.

Since the leader material is fairly stiff, the jigs tend to stay separated pretty well once they hit the water, and the rig really does the job, both in winter holes and in spring on the deeper grass.

This is not to say it's a pleasure to cast. Until you get the rhythm of it, you'll have jigs tangled in your guides, in your hat, everywhere. The trick is to make a fairly slow backswing instead of the quick snap we all love with a single lure. It's a little awkward, but, like marriage, you get used to it.

Tipping

Tipping with a small bit of shrimp or some Cotee Pro-Bait definitely increases the number of strikes you get in winter. This can be great if you're on a hole with mostly trout and reds, or it can be a pain if you've settled into pinfish alley. If there are lots of pins or catfish around, lose the tip--otherwise, use it, and you'll boost your catch.

Just remember to keep the tip small, no larger than a single section of shrimp or the small size of Pro-Bait. Larger chunks may actually put off the fish in winter, and they can ruin the action of small, light jigs.

Go light, go deep, go slow--but don't fall asleep. Those slow-moving lures can catch some awfully big fish if you stay alert.

CHAPTER 9

TROUT OF THE LONESOME LEG & THE PANHANDLE

"There's more good water here than you could fish in a year, if you only stopped once at each good hole," says guide Bill Roberts. You can believe it, too, looking at the map of Cedar Key, about a hundred miles north of Tampa, Florida.

There's no significant human habitation for 20 miles to the south and pretty well a hundred miles to the north, discounting a fishing village here and there. And every bit of that vast stretch is veined with blackwater creeks, salt marshes, palmetto woods and shallow grass flats.

Cedar Key

The town itself looks a lot like it has for the last 50 years, with bird dogs drowsing in the streets on weekday afternoons, and as many boats as pickup trucks parked in the driveways. Just about all of the 800 souls in town in one way or another makes their living from the rich estuary that spreads away seemingly forever into the oyster-laced back country. It's angling Valhalla, a complete anachronism in a state where growth has gone mad elsewhere.

Prime fishing gets rolling in early spring, about the time the wild ducks head north. Spring action is around the oyster bars and flats, where schools of big yellow-mouthed seatrout gather to spawn come April and May. A jig or a topwater plug dropped anywhere over the grass is likely to draw fish during this period, including a few big ones to 4 pounds, though the average trout here runs about a pound-and-a-half.

Shell bars like sprawling Corrigan's Reef, northeast of Cedar Key and Lone Cabbage, Half Moon and Suwannee Reefs to the northwest, are good for some larger trout in spring also.

Since redfish became gamefish several years ago, there has been excellent redfishing inshore around the holes, mangroves and oyster bars throughout the spring for anglers tossing jigs and gold spoons. It's not uncommon to nail a trout on one toss, a red on the next.

If you fish the deeper grass in spring, you'll also connect with Spanish mackerel with some regularity. They're part of a massive run that gathers at Sea Horse Reef, a spit of sand and grass jutting 10 miles into the deeper water, sometime in early April.

You can also pull some big trout from the reef, primarily on topwater plugs, in both spring and fall. And don't be surprised if a big mackerel crashes that act, as well--the larger ones love topwaters.

Fall action is good for everything, with trout and redfish at a peak in the back country creeks in October and November, mackerel hot at the reef, and grouper moving closer to shore to spawn. As the first freezes arrive, thousands of trout and reds crowd into the deeper creeks, and into the channels of the big Suwannee River, about 10 miles northwest of town.

The Suwannee

Trout fishing is particularly good in the Suwannee Delta, where Hog Island and several others split the flow into a number of channels ranging from 15 to 20 feet deep. When water temperatures drop into the low 60's and upper 50's, this is trout city.

The main bites usually take place in West Pass and East Pass, the two largest branches of the flow. The fish average big here, close to 3 pounds, and there are usually lots of them--as well as lots of anglers trying to catch them.

The trick in the main holes is to anchor, cast across the current or slightly downtide, and then hop your lure downstream with the current. This is effective because the trout are all facing into the tide, and it also helps avoid snags on the rocky bottom. (It's still a good idea to use 15-pound-

66

Fishing the oyster bars in Apalachicola Bay with flyrod streamers or topwater plugs can produce full-grown trout like this one. Top action is in fall.

test line and jigs with light wire hooks, so you can pull free when the inevitable snag occurs.)

Anglers tap the action by slow-hopping plastic-tailed jigs or bucktails in the 3/8 to 1/2 ounce range right on bottom, or dancing slow-sinking lures like the 52M MirrOlure just off bottom. Live shrimp or small baitfish are also effective.

There are also fish--and fewer boats--in some of the side creeks, including Bennet and May, and several that run through Hog Island. In general, anyplace you can find water more than 10 feet deep, you might find trout. (And lots of other stuff including reds, drum, sheepshead and mangrove snapper.)

The action remains good until it gets really cold in January, and usually things remain pretty flat through February before starting to perk again with the warming trends of March.

The endless pothole country also holds excellent populations of ducks most years, for those who want a combination hunting and fishing trip in late December and early January. It's always cold and frequently windy, but those who can find their way into the feeding areas before dawn can be assured of a mixed bag of fins and feathers.

The only catch in all this is that navigation in the area is difficult, to say the least. Though there are hundreds of square miles of shallow flats much like the Florida Keys further south, the water color ranges from coffee black to

Trout along the panhandle sometimes move out the passes and along the beaches when heavy rains turn inside waters muddy.

chocolate milk-stained. It's rarely clear enough to see bottom in more than a foot of water anywhere on the inside, so running by "reading the water" as you can further south is impossible. And there are oyster bars and rocks hidden like mines just about anywhere you want to go. This means you either have to hire a guide on initial visits, or use a boat without a prop.

What kind of boat has no prop? Airboats, of which you'll see plenty, and jet drives, of which you'll see a growing number. I took a Grumman Outlaw, an all-welded aluminum bass boat that floats in about 4 inches of water, powered with a Yamaha 80-horse jet, and ran the country like a pro, even though I had no idea where the channels were. If you don't have a jet or an airboat, and would rather find fish without a guide, plan on going slow and doing most of your traveling on rising water in case you get stuck. You can run the largest of trailerable boats offshore for the Spanish and grouper, because there's a deep, marked channel all the way from the city docks. But for backcountry trout fishing, a flat-bottomed jon boat of 16 feet or so or a shallow draft bonefish skiff are among the best choices.

Jetties like those at Destin and other panhandle passes can sometimes produce trophy trout like this one, taken on a Rat-L-Trap. (photo by Larry Larsen)

You don't really have to travel far from the docks to find action most of the time, however. Bill Roberts and his wife Anna Rae, also an excellent licensed guide, put me on several productive fall trout holes within casting distance of the fish houses along the access road, Route 26, which is the only way in and out of town.

Oyster Chum

One sure way of finding good fishing is simply to look for an oyster boat. According to Roberts, the hand-tonging and culling of oysters, practiced by dozens of skiff operators here throughout the cooler months, creates a chum line that draws trout, reds, and sheepshead where ever the boats stop. There are always small crabs hiding in the shells, and a few culled oysters inevitably get broken open by the oystermen's hammer as they knock the small ones apart from the larger keepers. If you anchor downstream from them and fish with live shrimp or jigs, you'll frequently find action. (Take along a box of crackers and some hot sauce, and buy a sack of oysters to munch on while you fish--they're some of the sweetest you'll find along the Gulf Coast.)

You don't even have to leave the docks to catch fish at times. The public fishing pier downtown spans some of the deepest water in the area as it stretches out into the dredged ship channel, and there are always trout, drum, sheepshead and other finny critters around the pilings.

Also downtown are some very good but pricey seafood restaurants and some other interesting side-attractions, if you don't happen to be a fishing addict. There's a good museum of early Florida artifacts, a fair number of curio and antique shops, and plenty of places where you can get baywood smoked mullet, the world's finest. It's all within walking distance of the little motels downtown, as is the city boat basin, where you can tie up without fear of wind or waves from any direction thanks to the almost completely landlocked harbor.

For more information, contact the Cedar Key Chamber of Commerce at (904) 543-5600. For reservations at the Cedar Cove Condominiums call (904) 543-5332.

Apalach And The Panhandle

Trout fishing along the panhandle ranges from fair to outrageously good, with Apalachicola Bay falling into the latter category, particularly in October and November when the shrimp are heading for the sea. Trout by the tons pour into areas like East Bay and the lower end of the many tidal creeks that make up the delta of the Apalachicola River, and hundred-fish days are still possible here. They don't often catch big ones, but when the bite is on, you can just about wear yourself out pulling them aboard. There are plenty of fish-camps, with boat rentals, available close to the action.

Other productive areas along the panhandle include the aptly-named Oyster Bay, accessed out of Spring Creek, Ochlockonee Bay and Alligator Harbor, and St. Vincent Sound, the west end of Apalachicola Bay. Very productive--and more like clear-water fisheries further south--is St. Joseph Bay, which is loaded with submerged grass and big trout that eagerly hit topwaters.

At Panama City, West Bay and North Bay are both good trout fisheries, with the fish running well up the deeper creeks in winter, out on the grass edges in spring and fall. Big Choctawhatchee Bay at Fort Walton Beach can be excellent at times--charters are available at Destin. Pensacola Bay and Perdido Bay are also fine fisheries, with strong surges in October and November and good action in the shallows in spring.

70

CHAPTER 10

ANCLOTE: THE LOST KEYS TO WEST COAST ANGLING

The Anclote Keys are the last of the Mohicans in the string of barrier islands that stretch along much of Florida's west coast, beginning at Sanibel, ending well north of St. Petersburg. And, as the northern terminus of that island chain, they're the last to offer the amenities of those further south, the white sand beach and the clear waters that so attract fish and fishermen.

At the same time, the area is the starting point for the broad, shallow grass flats that stretch northward throughout the "Big Bend" area around the horn to Apalachee Bay.

At Anclote, the 20-foot contour is less than two miles offshore, while just five miles north, off Port Richey, it's seven miles out. And by the time it gets to Homosassa, the 20-foot mark is 20 miles from shore. The islands represent a major habitat break, and like such areas everywhere, it teems with life as a result.

What's more, the Anclote area has remained productive thus far because development has taken its time working northward from St. Petersburg and Tampa, and though things are booming now, the best fishing areas are well away from the shore, so less subject to the problems of urban runoff, sewage outfalls and all the ills that human population brings.

The waters inside the islands, in Anclote Anchorage, are not nearly so clear as they once were, and scallops are getting hard to find there where they were once abundant, both signs of possible trouble ahead. But for the present, fish populations do not seem to have suffered.

71

The area is one of the best trout spots anywhere south of the Suwannee, a year-long magnet for Spanish mackerel, and a still untapped bonanza of redfish in the shallow flats and islands inshore. Bottom anglers find all the grouper they want within 15 miles of shore throughout the cooler months, and sometimes only minutes off the island, and big schools of king mackerel spend lots of time here in spring and fall.

The Grab Bag Approach

The area welcomes a potpourri approach, because the spots where you can catch trout also often produce a bit of everything else. My son and I spent a typical morning off the north end of the island recently and sampled a little of everything Anclote has to offer.

We started out at the edge of the grass flat, anchored in about 12 feet of water north of North Anclote. There's an obvious break line here, just west of Marker 4, where the grass ends and the white sand bottom of the open gulf begins, and it inevitably holds Spanish mackerel during the warmer months.

We put out a bit of encouragement in the form of a block of ground chum in a net bag off the stern cleat, and before long a cloud of pinfish and other small critters showed up to nibble on the goodies. We didn't pay much attention, though, until the swarm of small fish suddenly vaporized as the silver form of a mackerel arrowed through.

We both tossed out 1/8 ounce jigs with silver plastic tails, and both had instant hook-ups. We cranked in a pair of 16 inchers, put them in the box, and caught two more over the next 10 minutes, plus missing at least a dozen strikes. (Unfortunately, that's often the count when trying to hook mackerel on jigs.) That was it for the jigs--the mackerel around us had seen all they wanted of them.

But when I switched to a silver Rat-L-Trap and brought it buzzing along just under the surface, a 3-pound mackerel exploded on it. We got two more that way, then went back to the jigs to finish off our limit. (We used no wire on our lures-- the mackerel here generally won't touch a lure with wire attached. Thirty-pound mono does the job, eliminating most cutoffs, and drawing a lot more strikes.)

Slow-sinkers like the Rattlin' Flash work well in the clear waters off Anclote Key, although excessive grass can be a problem some days. Fish are caught anywhere from right against the mainland to 5 miles out over the vast grass beds.

Had the action been slower, we could have made the run to South St. Martin's Reef, about five miles north/northeast of Marker 2, where mackerel limits are usually a sure thing in April. There are also plenty of other unnamed shoals, most rising to about five feet in surrounding depths of 8 to 10 feet, where mackerel frequently hang out.

Deep Water Trout Flats

After that, we moved inshore about a quarter-mile over the thick grass, and began bouncing small, dark jigs right along bottom. The clear water here allows rich grass growth in up to 12 foot depths, providing thousands of acres of prime water to explore.

But as guide Everett Antrim, known locally as "Mr. Trout" points out, there are a whole lot of places where they ain't.

"You can drift along for hours getting a bite on only every 20th cast or so, and then all at once you hit a pod and catch a fish on every cast," says Antrim. "The trick is to get a feel for

A swimmer-tail jig like this Cotee--invented for Anclote area waters--is a prime lure for not only trout, but also the Spanish mackerel that abound there in spring, summer and fall.

those spots that hold schools a lot of the time, and to know how to find them on a daily basis."

Captain Dennis Royston, also a regular on these flats, notes that Loran or GPS electronic navigation gear is the easy way to pinpoint these spots, and it's highly effective for locating fish well north of Anclote Island.

"The flats near the island get hammered pretty hard simply because most people use the land and the nearby shoals and markers as landmarks. If you move a few miles north, you'll find trout that get a lot less pressure and are often more cooperative," says Royston. "Once you locate these spots and record the numbers on them, you can go back and catch trout with the loran, just as you do grouper farther offshore."

Trout, sea bass and the occasional flounder kept things interesting until my son and I drifted near the edge of the grass, where we again hooked a pair of mackerel, these quickly released.

The trout were most abundant over what local expert Steve Marusak calls "salt and pepper" bottom, where there

Castnets are used to collect sardines around Anclote Island, which are in turn used to capture big trout and snook around Anclote and nearby Honeymoon Island.

are numerous small patches of white sand scattered here and there throughout the grass. This is along the western edge of the grass bank in general, within a mile of the change to sand bottom.

Following Marusak's tips, we made sure the weedless jigs stayed in contact with the grass, dredging along just inches from the bottom. Another drift or two and we had all the trout we could use, so we turned inshore for reds.

In general, the reds here hang around the rocky points on high water, moving back into swash channels and bay necks as the water drops. These same channels and deeper pools also hold trout frequently, and a topwater plug like the Bangolure or a 7M MirrOlure will draw them out.

Spoil banks around the mouth of the Anclote River, Gulf Harbors, and the Pithlachascotee are good spots to look for both trout and reds, as are most of the bays north of Hudson. There are lots of oyster bars on the flats between Aripeka and Weeki Wachee, and these sometimes hold fish, too.

Guide Jim Bradley free-lines sardines on the deeper grass off Hernando Beach in late summer, and routinely catches and releases 50 to 100 trout per trip, including more than his share of 3 pounds and up jumbos.

Winter Hot Spots

The action is dependable throughout spring, summer and fall, and while the mackerel and kings disappear in November most years, there's usually a massive winter movement of lunker trout along with some reds, flounder and mangrove snapper, into the larger rivers like the Pithachascotee, the channels at Gulf Harbor, the Anclote River, and the hotwater outflow of the Tarpon Springs Powerplant.

In all of these locations, best action is usually with a live shrimp weighted with a bit of shot and drifted with the current near bottom. Small plastic-tailed Cotee jigs also do lots of business, as do slow-sinking plugs like the 52 M MirrOlure and the Bagley Finger Mullet.

A few snook are taken in spring in the deep water along the southern tip of Anclote Island, as well, and that's also a good place to pull a small planer with a little silver spoon to consistently catch spring mackerel. Area charter-boaters consider it a sure thing.

You can hit the snook or mackerel early, and then move inside the island to the grass to catch your limit of trout on 52M MirrOlures or small jigs on many days in spring and fall.

There are public ramps at Tarpon Springs and at New Port Richey, but both fill up early on weekends so you need to arrive shortly after daybreak to get a spot to park truck and trailer. Anclote Island itself is a state park, and a great place to picnic and swim when you need a break from fishing. There are also ramps at most of the villages further north, and these are generally less crowded.

CHAPTER 11

RITES OF SPRING
AT CHARLOTTE HARBOR

It was only perfect.

Jade water in from the Gulf on a soft riff of west wind, spreading like slow music over the sea grass plains and oyster bar mountains, whispering up beneath the edges of the mangrove forests, swelling like a spring blush on a young cheek to fill the flats and bayous and tide creeks, finding the deepcreek veins to the pulsing tideheart of Charlotte Harbor. Gulls cried far off, and pelicans fell like heavy stones into silvery fish explosions. Porpoises blew diamond breath, pah-whhhho-pah, into the painted, steaming dawn.

It was a morning to stand and look and hear, and not do anything else at all.

But, we had rods in our hands. Life in the doing, perhaps. We raised them, flexed them, sent bits of silvered plastic into the perfection. Stepped through the looking glass. Became part of the painting.

Tunnel-visioned as the pelicans now, eyes riding on the back of the flashing lure that turns, darts, skips, dives, seemingly at our will, without our conscious act. Frankensteinian fishers, we, our creation dances with the pulse of morning at the end of the lighted string--It's alive! It's alive!

So, too, think the yellow-mouthed, purple-backed trout, painted there also in the Created Perfection of the dawn. In a rush of black spots and gleaming flank, the first rises, as you know she must, having made the perfect presentation in the perfect spot on the perfect morning.

She is full of Spring, egg-rich, a solid block of promise, leaking yellow life as you hold her, tail just above the surface, the eggs slipping down into the tide, where the waste-not-want-not sea sends hurrying minnows to dine.

Let the first one go. You know it's right, somehow, without anybody saying anything.

The heavy woman-trout shakes her head, settles her ruffled dignity. She is tastefully gray and black again now, her skirts pulled down, a bit of water above her. She waddles off to make life happen.

Prime Time

There are days at Charlotte Harbor when God ought to charge admission.

And days when scalpers would raise the price.

Spring is particularly rich with these special days, beginning somewhere around the first of April and extending into June, when the big spotted seatrout appear from that great troutmine in the sky or where ever it is they hide the rest of the year.

You really won't need a calendar to tell you when the time is right. When the orange trees blossom at night and the mockingbirds sing you awake through the open bedroom window, and you wake up feeling like there's something, something... anything you ought to do except go to work, it's time.

Call in sick. Hitch up the boat. Go ahead. Life is short.

Finding The Fish

Charlotte Harbor is a great boot of a bay, with the angled ankle at Cape Haze. Though the footbone-is-connected-to-the-ankle-bone, that long spit of sand is a Mason/Dixon line, dividing the south bay from the north bay, two characters as different as gracious Georgians from laconic Vermonters.

The south end of the bay is mostly Gulf-fed, a clear-water fishery with broad, open grass flats butting up to deep green sounds where mackerel play.

The north bay is dark, tannin-fed from the Peace and the Myakka rivers, a bay of fringes, where dozens of bird-lined mud creeks lead off into mangrove nowheres.

78

Guide Larry Mendez is a master of taking big spring trout at Charlotte Harbor. Mendez relies on a combination of live sardines and artificials.

Both have good fishing, but in spring, the south bay is generally superior for trout fishermen. The mature trout come in from deep water wintering areas, or perhaps back out from the rivers and dredge holes and canals, to assemble on the flats for the rites of spring.

Where they so gather, some of Florida's finest topwater fishing occurs.

Some of the more productive spring areas usually include most of the flats nearest Boca Grande Pass and the open bay. Whether the fish gather on these grassy hills because the first whitebait of spring is there, or because it's their migration route, or their familial spawning area, they are usually there after the first new or full moon in April, on such banks as Jug Creek Shoal, which makes up off the northwest tip of Pine Island.

Moving along the north shore off that still-sleepy fishing town of Bokeelia, there are two dry shoals, each surrounded by a necklace of rich grass perhaps 100 yards wide in depths to five feet--prime water for big spawners.

Further east, the grassy basin at the entrance of Matlacha Pass, between Pine Island and the mainland, also produces. The flats east of Pineland and south of the channel toward Useppa Island can also be hot at times, as are the spoil islands and grass inside Captiva Pass.

On the north side of the harbor, the grass off the south shore of Devilfish Key also produces, as does the long basin stretching between the entry to Bull Bay and Turtle Bay--a good spot for large numbers of spring trout, if not for giants. The basin inside Sandfly Key, north of Devilfish, can also be good, and is also known for holding some spring tarpon.

Working the mile-long Cape Haze bar itself can also be good at times, so long as winds have not muddied the waters there. The bar is unfishable in winds over 10 mph, but good on calm mornings.

It goes on, of course, but we've already touched more than can be fished adequately in a week--so on to the method of the madness.

Quiet Baits For Quiet Waters

Of course, you can catch them on subsurface baits, but why would you want to? It's the difference between a ride in a convertible sportscar and a family sedan. Thrills, chills, explosions!

To the mechanics: there are surface lures, and then there are surface lures. The right surface lure depends on where you fish, and on wind and water conditions.

On those days when the water looks back at you, quiet baits are in order. Calm water requires a bit of decorum on the part of the plug, thus mannerly offerings like the Rapala, the Bomber Long A, the Rebel, the Thunderstick and the standard BangOLure are the ticket.

The floating Rat-L-Trap is also good, as is the 28-M MirrOlure. These are relatively small lures that work best with quick, short twitches that send out gentle rings--just enough to attract a trout's attention, but not enough to spook it in the clear, quiet shallows.

In the second circle of floaters are the prop baits such as the 5M MirrOlure (always with the front prop removed, of course) the BangOLure SP-5, Bomber Prop-A, the smaller

Topwaters like the Bangolure are unbeatable for taking trout over the grass at Charlotte Harbor. The clear water here makes it easy for the fish to see the floater, even in relatively deep water.

Devil's Horse, and the Heddon Torpedo. The Norman Rat-Lur, though not a prop bait, also fits in this middle category. These are for moderate wind conditions, where the surface has a strong ripple but is not rough. They create just the right amount of fuss, with the occasional loud splash, but more frequently just short darts and flashes that look just right to trout.

Finally, there are the big daddies of topwaterdom, such as the venerable Heddon Spook, the full-grown Devil's Horse, the Magnum Rapala, the Dalton Special, Rebel Pop-R and similars. These are big, obnoxious baits that will scare trout into Monroe County if fished in calm water--but on those rolly, rough days, bigger is better. They make a huge amount of fuss when worked hard, and they can be hard to work. Those who don't fish topwaters a lot will quickly find their wrists and forearms aching, and you may get "topwater elbow" after the trip.

Prospecting For Trout

Whatever the lure and the wind condition, whether the tide is coming or going doesn't seem to matter a great deal, but it must be moving vigorously to excite the fish. The flats that are active practically grab you by the lapels and shout

"Cast here!"--you see water swirling, baitfish jumping, birds diving.

Spring trout are schooling fish, so where you catch one nice one, you can expect to catch more. It's finding that first one that can sometimes be the problem.

The topwaters are a nice advantage in this, because many times they reveal fish that aren't really in a feeding mood. Spring trout frequently bat at floating lures without any real intention of eating them, as proven by the fact that they often get hooked in the back, side or tail. Or perhaps the idea is to first stun the bait and then eat it at leisure.

Whatever, when they come up in that chugging boil that sends your lure skyward, you know you're on fish. The chug of a trout is distinctive, sort of a hollow pop that sounds like no other species. If you restrain your first impulse to jerk the bait away from the fish, you can often draw a second, firmer hit, by just barely bobbing the lure, still in the same spot, just enough to impart a little life.

Teasing Trout To Take

Once you get a fish to make that first commitment, you can usually talk her and her companions into serious trouble. Try the same lure back to the same spot first. This time, bring it along slower, twitching and wobbling piteously, but without a lot of forward motion. This is accomplished by keeping the rod tip low, making the twitches short, and giving slack instantly after each.

All presentations should be with the current, or quartering it from downstream--that is, the lure ought to move with the tide, rather than against it. Fish always face into water flow--otherwise, they can't hold their position--so your lure needs to come from uptide for the fish to see it easily. Also, wounded baits always go with the flow, so you're making a more natural presentation with the tide.

Trout have a habit of gliding up within a few inches of a floating bait and then simply waiting there for it to make a move. You can often hesitate a second, then barely jiggle it and draw the strike.

Usually, that's all it takes, but after you've caught several the fish may wise up. Offer them something different to take

Scott Moore, on the conning tower, is perhaps the nation's most famed inshore guide. His favorite fishing spot? Charlotte Harbor.

a few more--a slow-sinker like a 52M MirrOlure or a Bagley Finger Mullet will do the job, as will a swimmer-tail jig in quarter-ounce size.

Catching big trout at Charlotte Harbor takes some of the same cautions required for catching snook, which is to keep the boat well back from the spot you're working, perhaps anchoring it for positive control, keeping a low profile, maybe to the point of getting out and wading on calm mornings, and using tackle that allows a long presentation. The jumbos are not only scarcer than smaller trout, they're also more wary, so it pays to be extra cautious.

Guys who consistently catch the larger fish often find them in shallower water than that normally considered trout water by the weekend angler. While the typical trout flat for 14- to 16-inch fish might be 4 to 6 feet deep, the biggest spring trout are often found on flats averaging 1 to 3 feet. Again like snook, the jumbos often settle into slight depressions in such water, perhaps only 6 inches deeper than the surrounding areas. They also like to wait on the edge of breaks in the flats, where the water makes an abrupt change from waist-deep to knee-deep. Toss your bait up on the shallow part, bring it wiggling back over the edge, and hang on.

Light tackle usually catches more fish than heavier stuff. You need a leader in Charlotte Harbor because there are always snook around, but keep it light--I personally like 18 inches of 20-pound-test Fenwick Saltline, but any low-vis mono in that range works fine.

Tie your plug on with a loop knot, a seven-times-around Uni or the MirrOlure loop or similars, so that it has extra action. Metal snaps are not a good idea on topwaters, because they weight down the nose and cut the action.

For baitcasters, use 12-pound running line, for spinners 8. These light lines allow for long casts, particularly important on those mirror-calm mornings. (It's not good to fish the larger plugs on 8, however, because the vigorous jerking quickly overstresses the line and makes it brittle. In general, baitcasters are called for if the lure weighs much over one-third of an ounce.)

Follow these suggestions and most mornings it doesn't take long to boat a limit. Then you can go off after the reds, which are schooling on the flats at this time, or snook gathering in the passes, or tarpon and mackerel ganging up off the beach. . . it might be a long time before you get back to the office.

CHAPTER 12

SARASOTA BAY

Out of sight, out of mind.

That's the way many anglers treat Sarasota Bay, the 15-mile long "little sister" to Tampa Bay and Charlotte Harbor. Though Sarasota Bay is only a short hop from either of the larger bays, few but local anglers ever make the trip.

Particularly in late fall and early winter, it's a trip well worth making, as Largo angler David Fairbanks discovered not long ago. Fairbanks, who is a noted light-tackle fisherman and holder of several International Gamefish Association world records for trout, redfish and snook, joined Jim Ising of Coastal Lures and myself for a morning on the upper end of Sarasota Bay, and came back singing its praises.

In about four hours that morning, we brought more than 40 trout to the boat. Fairbanks polished the day off by decking a pair of 28-inch snook, and everybody was on the way home by lunch. Not a bad morning, anywhere you go.

"The bay has a lot of deep, clear grass flats,," says Fairbanks, "and that kind of water is just what trout want when they're moving around in fall. They aren't up in two feet of water like they are in spring, and they haven't gone to the deep holes and rivers like they do on cold fronts. It's perfect holding water."

The bay is separated from the open Gulf of Mexico only by the thin barrier of Longboat Key, and is fed daily infusions of clear water with each tide change through Longboat Pass, New Pass and Big Sarasota Pass.

There are no major freshwater rivers flowing in to darken the water, and pollution, though a problem close to the downtown Sarasota area, has not become bad enough to cause massive algae growth and murky water. Thus, turtle grass thrives in water up to 6 feet deep, and here as elsewhere, turtle grass and sea trout go together.

Where To Fish

The north end of the bay, from the town of Cortez south to White Key, is particularly productive, because the entire area is a quilt-work of shallows, mangrove islands and spoil bars, regularly flushed with heavy tide flows from the deep channels of Longboat Pass.

The long bars that jut eastward from Whale Key and from Bishop's Point also produce, as do the flats in front of the John Ringling home. The shoals on the south end, around New Pass, are also highly productive at times.

Fairbanks suggests exploring these areas via a shallow-draft boat, seeking holes that are slightly deeper than the surrounding water. On the day of our trip, we fished a flat where the water averaged about 3 feet, but the fish were all concentrated in one basin about 100 yards long where the water dropped to 4 foot depths. That 1-foot change made all the difference--we caught nothing anytime we cast to shallower water.

There are also numerous canals and dredge holes in the area, as well as several deep creeks such as Phillipi, all good spots to try for both trout and snook when the water chills.

Finding the fish is a matter of drifting over likely areas and casting ahead of the boat. If you catch a fish or two on a drift, you motor in a wide circle around the area and return upwind for another drift.

The fish bite on either incoming or outgoing tides, but don't do much on slack periods according to David Fairbanks.

Techniques

Jim Ising had brought along a box full of his then-new "Rattlin' Flash" plugs, and naturally insisted that we give them a try.

The rattling version is a much-improved model of the original Hot Flash, a lure that has been homemade on the

Jim Ising of Coastal Lures unhooks a keeper. Slow sinking plugs fished on grass flats near the ICW produce well in fall and early winter.

East Coast for more than 50 years, mostly by hook-and-line commercial fishermen until recently.

Ising's new version, with a change in the balance and the addition of rattles in the head, is a quantum leap from the original.

It has a remarkable wobble when worked with the usual pumping action, and a tendency to dart and flash sideways, just like a wounded sardine. When it's cranked straight ahead, it swims with a very rapid wiggle, sort of like a Rat-L-Trap. And the two large weights in the head create just enough noise to get fish looking in the right direction. It's a sort of clicking sound that might imitate a shrimp.

The lure has enough weight to work at about 3 feet on a typical trout retrieve. Ising recommends that you wait about two counts after the lure hits water to allow it to sink slightly, then twitch the rod sharply, about a six-inch twitch, then take up slack, then make a couple twitches, then take up slack and so on.

"The thing never goes the same way twice," says Ising. "I think it works because it's so erratic, like a wounded bait."

On the day of our visit, the color that was most effective was a pink, blue and silver creation that Ising calls his "pinfish" pattern. It outfished other colors two to one, slightly changing my opinion that color doesn't make as much difference as lure makers would like us to believe.

Karl Wickstrom, conservation leader and publisher of Florida Sportsman Magazine, shows a Sarasota Bay whopper taken while fishing with Captain Johnny Walker. The fish grabbed a Zara Spook fished near a sandbar.

Other lures that work well on Sarasota Bay trout through the first freeze include the venerable 52M MirrOlure, the Bagley Finger Mullet, and the Rat-L-Trap. Plastic-tailed jigs are also effective, as is live shrimp and--the local favorite among top guides like Johnny Walker--live pigfish.

In the spring, lots of fish gather around the big bars that stretch out into the bay, and they readily hit topwaters then. There are also "blitzes" at times in spring and early summer when ladyfish, jacks, trout and other species go bananas chasing juvenile sardines, and these produce some bonanza catches.

You can find the fish by looking for diving gulls and pelicans, and catch them on small topwaters (the 28M MirrOlure is hard to beat) or on 1/8 to 1/4 ounce silver-tailed Cotee or Bubba jigs, or small Champ spoons. These feeding binges don't necessarily happen over the grass flats--sometimes they're right in the middle of the bay--so it pays to keep your eyes peeled for diving birds.

Scott Moore, the famed inshore guide who learned much of his expertise in the waters around Cortez, still does well in that area by fishing island points on moving tides with live sardines throughout the spring, summer and early fall.

Trout hang around the long bars that extend far offshore in Sarasota Bay in spring and summer, and readily rise to topwaters cast in these areas.

Moore also pulls plenty of fish out of the "yellow holes", the sand-bottomed depressions in the grass, averaging a foot or so deeper than the surrounding flats. Trout, snook and reds all love these locations. Fishing them effectively requires a quiet approach and long casts, but if you hit a half-dozen holes, it's almost sure that one of them will produce.

Trout fishing is not always easy on Sarasota Bay, anymore than it's always easy anywhere these days. But with a bit of patience and the right techniques, most anglers should be able to find action there that makes it worth a bit of travel away from the bigger, better-known sister bays north and south.

CHAPTER 13

SPRING CREEK TROUT

The Gulf Coast between Chassahowitzka and Crystal River is unique in Florida, an archipelago of mangrove islands and spring-fed creeks that create one of the most productive estuaries in the southeast. The waters here are particularly generous in spring, when trout move into the shallow flats and lower ends of these creeks to spawn.

In warm years, the event begins in March. It's more dependable after April 1, and continues until the first big rains of mid-June. During these pleasant weeks--usually warm, dry and calm--big female trout prowl the grassy shallows to feed and drop their eggs, and they're particularly susceptible to topwater lures.

The fish are likely to be found on the flats out to about four-foot depths, and inside the rivers and creeks as far up as the turtle grass grows. In some salty creeks like those leading into Chassahowitzka National Wildlife Refuge, this can be a mile inland, while in the larger rivers--the Crystal, the Homosassa and the Chassahowitzka--the large volume of fresh water usually moves the trout out when they get ready to spawn, even though they tolerate the fresher waters during winter when they seek warm-water refuges.

Spring Lures

The fish take all the usual trout lures, including slow-sinking plugs, small plastic and hair jigs, and spoons. Live shrimp and killifish drifted under a popping cork are also effective. But they're most fun to catch on topwater lures, and for those who know how to make the floaters dance, the action can be awesome.

Of course, they don't always get hold of the thing, which is surprising since most plugs sprout two or three sets of treble hooks. (How is it that these hooks can miss a trout that you want to hook, but never miss the opportunity to stick into jackets, towels, other rods--anything that comes within a foot of them inside the boat?)

Fortunately, if you learn to tease them a bit, you can often convert those first noisy boils into solid takes. The trick is, first, not to take it away from them by striking too soon, and second, to entice them back for another try.

For the first, don't set the hook until you actually see the fish take the lure down, or see or feel the line tighten. If you jerk at the first splash, you'll often skitter the lure away from the fish.

Second, when one misses, keep the plug right over her, and just barely wiggle it by twitching your rod. If that doesn't work, give it one sharp twitch, then let it sit still. The explosion usually isn't long in coming.

Work The Tide

There's strong tidal action throughout the area, and all plugs work best when cast uptide and allowed to drift back with the current. The fish expect their food to be coming from "upstream", whether the tide is going in or out, and this is particularly true in the coastal creeks and rivers where the flow is strongest. It's also effective on the flats, particularly around oyster bars that interrupt the flow, like the numerous bars in Crystal Bay, so take advantage of tide action where ever you can find it.

Though most trout anglers like to keep their boats moving in a continuous drift, you'll often improve your spring catches by staking out or slipping an anchor over the side when you roll up the first fish.

Though trout don't school so tightly in spring as in winter, it's still true that where you find one, you're very likely to find several more of similar size. The clear water on these flats

The islands of St. Martins Keys provide a beautiful backdrop for Captain Earl Waters to practice a bit of fly casting for trout and redfish. Exceptional water clarity here requires long casts and a low profile.

makes it essential to get the anchor over quickly and stay well away from the fish.

Hotspots

Some of the better areas to explore for trout, starting around Crystal River, include all of Crystal Bay between the main channel and the power plant spoil banks, an area of abundant bottom vegetation dotted with hundreds of oyster bars and cuts. The bottom vegetation here is not all turtle grass-there's a good bit of tall, kelp-like weed that grows all the way to the surface, and it provides good trout habitat, as well.

The spoil banks themselves are also good at times, and sometimes produce very large fish in the cuts. The mouth of the Salt River also produces. So do the very clear grass flats on the outside of St. Martin's Keys, though these waters require long casts to avoid spooking the fish. It's also very shallow, so you need a shallow draft boat and the ability to read the water, even to get into the prime areas. However, the bottom is hard in much of the region--bad for lower units, good for wading--be advised.

Near Ozello, the mouths of Fish Creek, St. Martin's River and the adjoining bays are good, though it takes careful operation to run a boat in this area due to the extreme shallows and the very hard bottom. Don't go into this backcountry with a boat that draws more than 12 inches, and don't go on a falling tide.

Near Homosassa, the mouth of the Little Homosassa, Sam's Bayou, and the flats off the sides of the main Homosassa Channel are often good, as is Green Key Swash. Fish the ridges in Homosassa Bay, in particular--fingers of shallows that jut up between deeper sloughs of 4 or 5 feet are usually good.

South of the Homosassa River, both North Channel and Mason Creek produce. So do Blue Bay and Porpoise Bay, but here again it takes local knowledge and a very shallow-draft boat to avoid tearing up your lower unit.

Chassahowitzka Bay around Buckhorn Key and Bird Island can be very good in spring. Trout action is often good as far out as the "bird racks" several miles offshore, and the usually-clear water here makes it possible to successfully fish topwaters in up to 8 feet. (You're likely to catch some gag grouper around the many rockpiles in this area, too, and maybe run into a school of fast-moving bluefish as well. Keep your plugs clear of the blues, though, because their teeth will butcher them.)

There are numerous other areas that might produce in spring, and every angler with a few years of experience has his own "secret spots". Explore, do a lot of casting, and you'll soon find a few of your own.

Fishing The Muds

A unique phenomenon in this area is fishing the "muds" that develop during the November migration of shrimp seaward. At this time, thousands of fish gather to feed on the massed crustaceans moving from the grassy inshore nurseries to the offshore waters. During the day, the shrimp burrow into the bottom for protection, and the fish descend on them

Typical trout from the area are 14 to 16 inches long, though fish weighing up to 6 pounds are taken occasionally. In winter, a run of very large fish sometimes shows up at the Crystal River Powerplant.

and root them out, creating huge muds that may be a mile wide and 5 miles long at times.

The action is usually found just beyond the edge of the deepest grass, in 10 to 14 feet of water, beginning about 8 to 9 miles off Homosassa. Some years, the muds are rare and brief, some years they are abundant and last for weeks.

If you happen to be in the right place at the right time (trolling spoons for fall Spanish is a good way to cover the water as you look for the mud) you'll see a whitish discoloration at the surface, and a clear edge where the clear green water of the gulf meets the murk.

There are also likely to be fish breaking on top, and gulls diving from overhead.

This marks an amazing aggregation of fish below. And I do mean amazing. Once in my guiding days, I took two clients out to a mid-November mud and we caught, by actual count, over 550 mixed trout, ladyfish, pinfish, grunts, sea bass, snapper, gag grouper and Spanish mackerel. My hands had fish poisoning for weeks afterward.

Normally, the muds are not as good as that one, but if you hit a sizable mud, you can depend on very fast action indeed.

For most species in the murk, all you need is a 1/4 ounce jig with a gray, pink or white plastic shrimp tail. You cast it out, let it sink, and raise the rod into whatever fish gets to it

Oyster bars are good spots to try on rising water. Fish the cuts nearby with small jigs, or drift a topwater over the bar itself on high.

first. If you don't get a bite, give it a sharp hop or two and you'll connect.

If you want to really make things happen, add a bit of cut shrimp or Cotee Pro-Bait. This is particularly helpful in drawing strikes from mackerel, but it also increases the number of pinfish you catch.

(Incidentally, the mackerel seem to hang on the edge where the clear water meets the mud. They often hit best if you cast into the milky water and then bring the jig out very fast into the clear. If there are big ones around, they will also eat the trout you try to crank in from this edge area. And don't be surprised if an occasional king mackerel comes along and eats a trout or even a small Spanish).

Added bonuses of fishing this area are the remarkably large and beautiful saltmarshes that lead out to the bays, and the still-quaint river towns and fish camps where you launch. All that, plus you don't have to rinse out your motor when you get home--the fresh spring water flowing down the rivers does the job for you. Go in June and you can dive up a mess of scallops after the morning trout bite. MacRae's Bait House is the center of fishing and culture at Homosassa--good rooms, good tackleshop, good tall tales at day's end. The number there is (904) 628-2602. At Crystal River, Knox Bait House, (904) 795-2771, is the place to put in.

CHAPTER 14

TAMPA BAY AND THE
WEST CENTRAL COAST

Florida's central Gulf Coast shows the good, the bad and the ugly of trout fishing, with action ranging from spectacular to putrid depending on the amount of environmental destruction in the particular piece of water you happen to fish.

Tampa Bay is the largest estuary in the area, and a microcosm of what's left along this whole stretch of coast. The big bay has lost almost half of its sea grass and over 80 percent of its historic mangrove stands as a result of 50 years of development, and for creatures as habitat-sensitive as seatrout, it can probably never be what it once was.

On the other hand, improvements in wastewater treatment and restrictions on new construction have definitely made improvements in water quality, and sea grasses are growing once again in areas where they haven't been seen in years. Trout restoration is likely to follow--provided severe harvest limits are put in place in order to give the fish a running start, ala the redfish restoration of the late 1980's.

Hillsborough Bay

The bay is really three bays, Hillsborough on the northeast, Old Tampa Bay on the northwest, and Tampa Bay proper to the south, which connects both smaller bays with the gulf. Hillsborough Bay is the most polluted, and consequently offers the least trout action--but it can produce well at times.

The mouth of the Alafia River, near Gibsonton, is a noted spot for trout to gather on the first cold fronts of late

97

November, and anglers working jigs and small spoons around the spoil islands there regularly make good catches.

Also good during this time is the mouth of Bullfrog Creek and the adjacent area known as "The Kitchen" by locals. The dredge holes just north of the Big Bend Powerplant are gathering spots for trout when the water gets really cold, as are all the ship basins and the hotwater outflow of the plant itself, with fishing remaining good in these areas on jigs worked deep and on live shrimp well into January. (There's lots of flow out of these powerplants on cold mornings when the generators are running full blast. It often pays to lightly weight a shrimp or a killifish, toss it up current and let it drift back, repeating the motion again and again over likely water, rather than letting the bait sit still on bottom. The largest trout--as well as snook--seem to take the bait much better if it moves with the flow.)

The lower Little Manatee River produces lots of trout in fall and winter as well, and there's usually a big surge of spring fish into the deep holes off Shell Point in March and April.

My angling pal (and attorney) Robert Foster of Tampa showed me several old boat wrecks around this portion of the bay, and each of them is usually good for a whopper trout up to 5 pounds if you happen to be the first boat to visit that day. Big trout seem to home in on this sort of isolated structure in deep water--find your own wreck or rockpile in 8 to 10 feet of water and you may connect.

Tampa Bay Proper

The broad flats stretching southward from Shell Point to Port Manatee are good for topwater action from spring through fall, and a good place for mixed-bag action on trout, reds and snook for wading anglers. There's often a big push of trout into Cockroach Bay in spring and fall, as well, and this clear, shallow bay is a great topwater spot.

Beyond the Sunshine Skyway on the south side, broad flats open from the mouth of the Manatee River (itself a good winter trout spot) and provide excellent topwater action all the way to the ICW, which runs between Anna Maria Island and the mainland. The clear flats range from 1 to 4 feet deep and are often loaded with sardines--a good spot for a sardine imitation such as the Rat-L-Trap or the 28M MirrOlure.

FCA leader Richard Seward wades a favorite flat on Old Tampa Bay. Seward often finds fish in "channels" that are only three feet deep, and barely a foot deeper than surrounding waters.

The flats on the northwest side of the Skyway, extending to Fort DeSoto and surrounding Bunce's Pass, are frequently good for drift fishing action on trout. There are also occasional runs of jumbo trout along the beaches in this area and at Egmont Key, particularly where rockpiles break the surf.

The deeper grass flats off Pinellas Point can produce. This is an area with strong tide flow due to the deep channel from Pass-A-Grille and Bunce's Pass, plus lots of bait and lush turtle grass bottom. For waders, the Clam Bar that extends in a broad arc off the northeast side of the Sunshine Skyway causeway is a good place to toss topwaters. If you're looking for a charter in this area, you can't do better than Captain Paul Hawkins--see the chapter on guides for his number.

On the south side of the main Tampa Bay entrance, Terra Ceia Bay (stomping grounds of noted guide James Wood) is accessed via a deep channel between Rattlesnake Key and Snead Island, just north of the Manatee River entry. The bay has some pollution problems, but can provide excellent drift fishing in fall for school trout.

Old Tampa Bay
In Old Tampa Bay, the flats and channels around Double Branch and Rocky Creek produce in early winter. This is a

Slow-sinking plugs like the Rattlin' Flash and baitcasting reels like the Shimano Calcutta are favorites in many parts of Tampa Bay.

favored wading area for many top anglers like Florida Conservation Association leader Richard Seward, a former commercial hook-and-line trout fisherman .

Also good are the grass patches on the south side of Courtney Campbell Causeway--another favorite area for boatless waders--and on the southeast side of the Howard Frankland Bridge. South of the Gandy Bridge, the flats of Weedon Island are often good, as are the backwaters that wind through the mangrove islands and residential canals of Smacks Bayou and Coffeepot Bayou. Captain Russ Sirmons is master of fishing this piece of water.

St. Pete To Clearwater

Though the beaches north of Tampa Bay are some of the most intensively developed real estate in Florida, the inside waters here continue to produce good trout fishing due to the regular infusions of clear water and bait from the gulf through the many passes.

Sardines are a favorite bait on much of Tampa Bay. They're chummed into range, then castnetted. Note the large, flow-through well--essential to keeping the delicate baits alive.

IGFA-record-holder David Fairbanks regularly takes lunker trout by working the first bars inside the passes on rising water with slow-sinking plugs like the Rattlin' Flash. The bays along the sides of the ICW are not broad here, but the water is fairly clear except on busy boating weekends, and the action can be steady for anglers who explore and find the larger grass patches.

The area is excellent in winter because thousands of trout (and snook, as well) move into the residential canals, and can readily be caught around the dock lights at night on free-lined shrimp or small DOA shrimp imitations.

Clearwater To Anclote

St. Joseph Sound provides plenty of shallow, clear water here, much of it grassy, and thus there are plenty of trout in the area from spring through late fall, and all winter if temperatures are moderate.

The fish trade back and forth between the flats and the holes with changing temperature. In moderate weather, the edges of the spoil banks near the ICW are good places to throw topwaters like the Bangolure SP-5 for large fish--and some of these same jumbos are caught in the ICW itself on cold mornings in December and January, usually on live shrimp or jigs fished near bottom.

St Joseph's is the first open water directly accessing the gulf north of St. Petersburg, and is the beginning of the vast grass flats that extend all the way around the curve of Florida to the Panhandle Beaches. It's a unique transition zone, and like such habitat changes everywhere, uniquely productive.

In short, despite all the urbanization and a population approaching 2 million, the Bay Area has a whole lot of trout fishing, probably more than you can sample in one lifetime.

CHAPTER 15

FLORIDA'S EAST COAST
AND THE EVERGLADES

The bulk of Florida's trout fishing is done on the West Coast, but that doesn't mean there are not plenty of avid trout-aholics along the Atlantic shore. From The Georgia border south to Stuart, and around the corner through the Everglades, trout are avidly sought and steadily caught in this area, and in one section, the Indian River, the biggest of all seatrout are found, a strain onto themselves, which grow faster and live longer than trout in any other estuarine system.

East Coast

There's a fine run of big trout into the lower St. Johns in fall and early winter. It's primarily deep-water fishing with jigs or live shrimp, but if you hit a school, you can readily set on one spot and catch your limit of fat keepers. The trick is to find a jetty, bar, rockpile or a deep side creek where the trout can gather out of the current and away from boat traffic--a depthfinder helps some, local knowledge helps a lot more. Check with area baithouses for the current hotspot and keep a steady eye out for ship traffic if you fish near the main channel. The side creeks both north and south of the St. Johns off the ICW are frequently good.

There's good fishing inside every inlet southward to New Smyrna, with fish usually found around the mouths of the many salt rivers that make off the bays and the Intracoastal Waterway. Deep, shell-bottomed holes are good throughout the area in late fall and early winter. There's a lot of good

103

fishing around the ICW bridges after dark, for those who suspend lights just off the water, as well.

At Mosquito Lagoon, the ICW spreads out and becomes trout Valhalla. You can put in at the venerable Oak Hill Fish Camp here and fish south for many miles, working the cuts between the spoil bars for jumbos, the deeper grass east of the ICW for numbers. There are many areas where the deep grass shoals rapidly to shallows here, and when the finger mullet are up on these edges, you can do no wrong with a topwater like the 5M MirrOlure. Fishing is good from April through November, and into January if you find the right section of the ICW where the fish are schooled to avoid the cold.

The legendary Indian River begins just beyond the Haulover Canal connecting to Mosquito Lagoon. Flats, spoil bars and points throughout the area produce in spring and fall, while the deeper central portions plus deep side canals are best in winter. Many big trout are taken around residential docks in cold weather, most by free-lining a shrimp or mud-minnow under the cover.

The Banana River, which runs parallel to the Indian River and passes through Cape Canaveral, is even better than the Indian River. The water is exceptionally clear, which this portion of the Indian River no longer is due to boat traffic and pollution, and the grass flats are lush.

That's the good news. The bad news is that you can no longer run a powerboat above the S.R. 528 Causeway, because the area is a manatee preserve. But some say that's good news, too, because fishing pressure has dropped to zero in the area. For those willing to wade or paddle a canoe, this stretch of the Banana River may offer the best trout fishing left on the East Coast. Topwaters are great worked around the spoil islands early and late, while drifting the deep grass at mid-day with jigs or slow-sinking plugs does well for keepers.

(The area is becoming famous for giant--and I do mean GIANT--redfish, as well. Guide Shawn Foster has been connecting with reds up to 50 pounds in water only knee deep. It's a great combo trip in fall or spring.)

The Indian River runs all the way south to the St. Lucie Inlet, and it averages a couple miles wide and about 4 feet deep for most of that length. This is the area where all the

The Banana River is exceptionally clear, and the grass flats are lush.

historic catches of giant trout came from, the area where a separate strain of fast-growing giants has evolved, and where there are still more big trout than in almost any other part of Florida. Pollution and overfishing have greatly reduced the catch of big fish in the last 15 years, but there's always the opportunity for a lifetime trophy, and rules now in the works could bring the fishery back in a few years.

The fishing techniques are much like those described above. Many anglers run the edges of the flats, looking for schools of mullet, and then pole or wade around those schools because the big trout frequently hang close. Grassy areas near the big inlets are always worth prospecting, as are the edges of the many spoil bars near the ICW.

Some strong schools of trout are caught well up the St. Lucie River in winter, and up the Loxahatchee, inside Jupiter Inlet, during the same period.

Trout fishing can also be good in Lake Worth, adjacent the Lake Worth Inlet, in the channels in winter, and on the few grass patches remaining in spring and fall.

The Everglades

Though most anglers who head for the Everglades have snook and tarpon on their minds, the waters here are also very good for trout. Fishing can be strong every month except in the dead of summer, when the area is just about too hot for anglers anyway, and definitely has too many skeeters and no-see-ums for any except crazed snook anglers.

105

Water adjacent any of the outside channels attract schooling fish in considerable numbers. It's possible to catch 50 or more trout as fast as you can cast when you hit one of these schools. Small gold or silver jigs and 2-inch-long silver spoons are the best lures. Diving terns usually reveal the hotspots.

Though the 'Glades are famed for their inside fishing, most trout are caught on the outside, where the clearer waters of the Gulf meet the tannin-stained water creeping down the jungle rivers.

Here as elsewhere, trout are likely to be most abundant where the water is clear enough to support turtle grass on the bottom. Find the grassy areas outside any of the major jumping off spots, in water 4 to 7 feet deep, and you'll soon find trout by drifting and casting a jig or slow-sinking plug ahead of the boat.

Some of the good areas for this include Cape Romano, Gullivan Bay, the mouth of the Fakahatchee River, the flats west of Indian Key, those around the passes and islands out of Chokoloskee, the flats east of Pavillion Key, at the mouth of the Chatham River, on either side of the Lostman's channel, and in Ponce de Leon Bay. Also good at times are roving schools around each of three points on Cape Sable. On low water, the channels out of Flamingo, including Joe Kemp and Snake Bight, are good for trout and a bunch of other stuff. On high, the flats around these cuts are good--fish the "potholes", which are sand blowouts a foot or so deeper than surrounding grass--they often hold trout.

106

Trout fishing is good year-around on the East Coast, but steady success requires a knowledge of the seasonal movements from flats to rivers and channels.

Also, in the water adjacent any of the outside channels, you may run into a trout/ladyfish blitz in spring or fall, as the fish school in considerable numbers to chase glass minnows. If you can get away from the ladyfish, it's possible to catch 50 or more trout as fast as you can cast when you hit one of these schools. Small gold or silver jigs and 2-inch-long silver spoons are the best lures. Diving terns usually reveal the hotspots.

In fall and winter, action is still good on the outside in moderate weather, and a lot of fish move into the backcountry if it gets chilly. Whitewater Bay is often good, as is Chokoloskee Bay and Fakahatchee Bay. The deep backcountry creeks often hold winter fish, particularly around shell bars on the rise, and around areas where little creeks drop into big ones on the fall. These are good topwater spots, and you're likely to catch snook on them as well as trout. A jig in the same waters will catch plenty of reds.

CHAPTER 16

GULF COAST TROUT
ALABAMA TO TEXAS

Trout fishing is good throughout the northern Gulf and around the horn into Mexico, with the abundance of the species depending largely on the availability of estuarine-type habitat. Alabama and Mississippi both boast some fine fishing inside their bays and barrier islands, but because the length of their coastlines is limited, so is the number of areas where trout are found. That can't be said of their neighboring states westward however.

Texas-sized Trout

Texans take their flats fishing very seriously, and jumbo trout are perhaps their favorite pursuit.

Trout are found in waters ranging from the deep ship channels at Corpus Christi to the murk of Galveston Bay, but the area most dear to the trout anglers' hearts is the Laguna Madre, a thin and narrow sheet of water stretching out more than a hundred miles inside the ring of barrier islands that jewel the Texas coast between Corpus and Brownsville.

The waters are shallow, generally clear, rich in grass and baitfish, and loaded with both trout and redfish.

One of the anglers who knows how to get them best is guide Doug Bird of Corpus Christi.

Bird runs some 40 miles from the nearest boat ramp to get away from weekenders, who he feels catch off growing trout before they can become trophies. He keeps a spacious camp on the Laguna, far down in the coyote country bordered by massive Kenedy County, so that anglers don't have to go and come in the same day. You tote your groceries, ice, gas--everything you're going to need, because there are no stores down there, and no people either except those in the other fishing shacks along the water.

The fishing can range anywhere from good to fabulous, depending on the weather and on the previous winter. If a big cold front caught the flats early the year before, it's likely that fishing for jumbo trout will be slow, because the Laguna is a natural trap where gator fish die by the thousands when a Blue Norther blows in. A major kill can knock back the population of trophy fish for several years.

On the other hand, a few years of moderate winters followed by warm springs can create bonanza fishing. Texas allows no net harvest of trout at all, so the only fish taken are those fooled by anglers' wiles. This results in lots of trout, and plenty of big ones, when Mother Nature smiles.

The anglers may either drift the shallows in flats rigs--including the strange-looking "flats scooters" that will run in only 4 inches of water--or step overboard to wade. More often than not, the best anglers wade because this allows a close approach to big fish without the danger of spooking them.

The usual techniques favored by trout anglers everywhere work well here, with topwaters particularly successful.

Texas anglers are also well aware of the effect of the spoon on trout--it's a favorite among many of the best. They also like long-tailed jigs like the Kelly Wiggler, with the plastic body about twice the length of that used in Florida and other East Coast trout depots.

Night Fishing

Night fishing is a major industry along the Laguna channel, and Doug Bird works hard at it in his camp. He runs powerful spotlights (powered by a diesel generator since you're 40 miles from the end of the electrical lines) over the waters at his dock to attract fish after dark.

In winter, the lights work especially well, often attracting sizable schools of monster trout that stack like cordwood in the flow of the tide. They won't always bite, but when they decide to hit, the action is furious. Free-lined live shrimp is usually the best bait.

110

Texas anglers like guide Doug Bird catch loads of big trout from the Laguna Madre on topwaters, spoons and long-tailed jigs.

Surprisingly enough, the trout can be remarkably selective at times , even when they're piled under the lights. One visit I made in October saw hundreds of trout jammed around Bird's dock as soon as it got dark, but the fish were eating only tiny minnows about an inch long. They ignored both live shrimp and conventional jigs, to our incredulity, behaving as perversely as dock snook in Florida waters.

We finally started trimming down the plastic tails of 1/8 ounce Cotees to try to imitate the natural. When we cut away the body to the point that it covered only the shank of the hook, with no overhang at all, the trout started to take. We caught more than 30 fish in short order, but without the surgery we would have caught none. Don't let anybody tell you trout are never finicky after dark.

Another location on the Texas coast noted for whoppers is the Texas City flats, near Galveston. Gerald and Viola

111

Texans fish remote stretches of the laguna from fish camps that are often 40 miles or more from the nearest town. The camps include generators to operate lights and refrigeration.

Hernandez set three line class records there in two months-- October and November--in 1984. Biggest was Viola's 14-pound, 6-ounce lunker on 8-pound test, which also happens to be the biggest spotted sea trout ever caught, anywhere, by a woman. The flats are part of Galveston Bay, largest on the Texas Coast.

Some nice fish are also caught in the numerous passes along the coast, and on the adjacent beaches. Other bays noted for producing fine trout fishing include Matagorda, out of Port Lavaca and surrounding towns, Espiritu Santo, in the same area, and Aransas Bay, in the Rockport area. With the exception of Corpus Christi and Galveston, there are no large cities on the Texas coast, and many of the remote stretches see very little fishing pressure at all--it's a real frontier for flats anglers used to the high-density angling in much of Florida these days.

The Chandeleurs

The Chandeleur Islands are a part of Louisiana, but the easiest way to get to them is to head due south from Biloxi or Gulfport, Mississippi. It's about a 25-mile run across the open

Anglers carry jonboats aboard larger mother ships to fish the Chandeleur Islands, off the Mississippi Coast. A number of charter operations offer these services.

Fishermen also fly to the Chandeleurs. Schools of fish can sometimes be spotted from the air. Float planes land in the sound behind the island.

Gulf to reach the crescent of sand that makes up the first outrider of the Mississippi River Delta, but the ride is more than worth it when things are right--this unique area looks like something displaced from the Florida flats, with white sand beaches backed up by broad, clear shallows loaded with turtle grass--and trout. There's no human habitation on the vast sweep of this sand bank, and the only people you see out there are other anglers.

A number of charter services operate out of Mississippi ports, and most provide a mother ship 80 to 100 feet long for lodging and smaller boats for fishing. You can also charter planes in coastal towns of Mississippi for the short flight--and since there's such good fishing along the beach, you may not need a boat at all. Some operators fly the surf until they see a school of fish (not hard to do when winds are moderate and the water is clear) then set the plane down on the beach or on floats in the flats and let you have at them.

While there's always good action for small to medium-sized trout over the grass flats behind the islands, lunker hunters beach their boats at the edge of the flats and hike across the narrow islands to fish the surf, particularly around areas where channels run through into the back country. Fish of five pounds and up are the rule in the surf, and the 10-pounder is always a possibility, especially for those who bring

114

Monster trout like this 10-pounder are sometimes taken in the surf in front of the Chandeleurs. Best bait for the giants is live finger mullet, which can be castnetted in the surf.

a cast net and free-line live mullet in the waves. (The same technique also accounts for plenty of big redfish--but watch out for sharks--there are usually plenty of them, so don't wade in too deep.)

The Chandeleurs are a remarkable and unique gift from Nature, and one that ought to be on the travel itinerary of every confirmed trout addict for at least one visit before he passes on to that great grass flat in the sky. Or maybe the Chandeleurs ARE that place, right here, right now.

Louisiana Trout

Louisiana offers a picture of what trout fishing used to be. It's one of the few places left where hundred-fish days are still routine, even though you can no longer keep all those fish thanks to progressive conservation laws, and it offers such a diversity of habitat that most who have sampled it agree, the Bayou State is the ultimate for the year-around trout-aholic.

Though not the most picturesque country, the flat, muddy bayou country south and west of New Orleans offers the most

115

spectacular fishing, particularly in October and November when absolutely incredible numbers of "specks" jam into the back country. Fishing is remarkably good pretty much every month except January and February.

Terry Shaughnessy, a former NFL linebacker who runs one of the leading guide operations in the western part of the state, reports that catches of 50 fish per angler per day are pretty much a given around Lake Calcasieu, a big saltwater bay southwest of the city of Lake Charles, until the water gets really cold. If you time it right, you can have a banner morning on the amazing number of ducks that funnel down the Mississippi Flyway, go home and eat a hot breakfast and be back on the water in time to catch a limit of trout (and redfish) before noon.

Shaughnessy says April through June is the best time for jumbo trout, July through September is best for those hundred-fish days, and October through December is the time for mixed-bag action on trout and reds. Accommodation, meals and guide service at Shaughnessy's Hackberry Rod & Gun Club are about $250 per day, total, for fishing, more for hunt/ fish combos.

Jigs including the Berkley Power Grub and Power Shad are the favorites, but sinking plugs including the Rat-L-Trap, 52M Mirrolure and Rattlin' Flash also work well.

The water is dark and murky, and baits with plenty of flash and sound--like the chrome Rat-L-Trap--are often the best choice. Most anglers work the 'Trap with a pumping action much like a jig, and also like a jig, the lure usually gets inhaled on the drop.

There are numerous creeks and bays winding through the area, and occasional locks crossing these flows. Where the water spills over is often a hotspot, particularly in summer when fish get both oxygen and food from the turbulence. Shaughnessy also catches a lot of fish from Sabine Wildlife Refuge during months it's open to fishing--it's closed as a haven for ducks and geese in fall and winter. These backcountry fish average 1 to 3 pounds, and are often mixed with lots of "white trout" or silver trout, which scale about a pound. When the fish are in the marshes, topwaters work

116

well, with the Tiny Torpedo one of the best. Flyrod poppers also work very well at times.

The many jetties in the area, where the delta country meets the Gulf of Mexico, also produce amazing quantities of both trout and reds. These structures of jumbled rock provide a haven for bait and are usually found adjacent deep water, so they're likely spots much of the year. And the inshore oil rigs, some many miles from shore in the shallow bays, can also offer spectacular action, and often some jumbo trout. Fishing centers include Venice, where guide Ronny Gronier fishes the backwaters of the mighty Mississippi itself, Grand Isle at the mouth of big Barataria Bay, and Lake Calcasieu.

There's also great inside fishing in the huge bays north and east of New Orleans, Lake Borgne and Lake Pontchartrain, during much of the year. The fish usually school up in deep water and you can expect company over them, but the action is steady.

In fact, it's hard to put your finger on a spot anywhere in southern Louisiana where trout are not within pirogue distance much of the year.

CHAPTER 17

GEORGIA AND THE CAROLINAS

The low country of Georgia and the Carolinas is a different world for anglers used to the grass flats and clear waters of Florida and the Gulf states. From the broad, green sweep of the Marshes of Glynn to the big blackwater sounds of North Carolina, this fertile estuary is a trout factory extraordinaire--but only for those who understand the tricks of a whole new way of fishing.

Georgia

"You can forget grass flats along the Georgia coast," says Georgia DNR biologist Spud Woodward. "The bottom is all mud and the water is frequently mud soup--grass just can't grow here."

No grass--but still loads of trout, in direct contradiction of what trout anglers have discovered in most other areas where trout abound.

"The rivers make the sounds very fertile," says Woodward, "but they also make them muddy. We have huge tides here, up to 9 feet around the new and full moons, and all that water pouring in and out over the mud bottom turns things so cloudy that the fish literally can't see a foot in front of them. So most of them don't even try to feed on these spring tides, and most fishermen know that. They stay home on the big tides, and go on the minimum flows in between."

This, you'll note, is directly opposite of the way many anglers plan their trips around much of the Gulf of Mexico, where a "big" tide is 3 feet. The plan of many Florida anglers is to hit the new and full moon tides, because lots of water and

119

lots of bait floods the flats on those periods--fish usually feed heavily.

There are other differences, as well. Light tackle is not often useful in the big Georgia rivers, says Woodward.

The best anglers have found that the most effective way to catch these trout is to drift a shrimp to them, and they do that by taking advantage of the moving water and floats 8 to 10 inches long. The line is run through the center of the float, with a stopper to allow bait and weight to sink near bottom where it drifts suspended with the tide.

The bait may be drifted 50 yards or more down a bank.

"When you have that much line out, there's a lot of slack and if you use light gear, you can't pick up that slack. So most fishermen use baitcasters, 15-pound-test line and 8-foot rods to do the job," says the biologist (and enthusiastic leisure-time angler).

Woodward says the big rods are used to sweep up the slack when the cork goes down, much like bass anglers use long, oversized rods to fish live shiners.

"It's odd, but these fish are sensitive to boats getting too close to them, even with the muddy water," says Woodward. "I've seen cases where anglers try to move in on them, and every time they drift their boat 10 yards closer, the trout move 10 yards downtide to keep their distance."

He said that some anglers dress their lines with fly-line flotant to keep it from sinking. The line floating on top of the water is easier to keep taut and easier to lift off the surface on the strike. Most use the small-diameter Kahle hooks for easy penetration.

Since there's no grass to draw the fish, they orient to shell bars, shoals and creek mouths during the warmer months.

"Basically, you want a falling tide at the creek mouths and cuts, because the fish will stack up there to take the shrimp and baitfish being sucked out of the marshes," says Woodward. "On the rise, they're likely to be around the shell bars where they can trap food against the edges. Sometimes, on these bars, they'll stay there through the tide phases, just changing sides as the tide changes. As long as the water clarity remains decent, they'll bite."

Trout reach considerable size at the northern limits of their range. Grub-type jigs are favorites in the coastal rivers in late fall and winter, but live bait is superior in spring, summer and early fall.

Seasonal Changes

Georgia trout spend their summers in the sounds and bays created where the rivers meet the Atlantic, and sometimes along the beaches.

Fall is bonanza time here, as the shrimp move down into the estuaries and the trout move up. Where they meet, it's trout fishing pandemonium, with hundred-fish days not at all uncommon from September through November.

"We have a 25 fish limit here, and during the fall if you get on just the right spot with clear water and moderate tides, you can catch that in an hour," says Spud Woodward.

The boom continues till Thanksgiving most years. After that, the shrimp have all migrated offshore, and the trout have gone far up the rivers to settle into deep holes where the water provides an insulating blanket. The fish travel as much as 8 miles inland during the period from late November through February, sometimes entering water that is completely fresh.

Shrimp is a good bait in the wintertime, but can rarely be purchased because few Georgia shrimpers operate then. Most anglers instead rely on grub-type jigs and slow-sinking plugs, which work well so long as they're worked slow and deep on moderate tides.

An unusual way of fishing is to seek out the black mud flats on sunny but cold winter days. On low water, these flats soak up the heat of the sun. As the water rises, they form patches of warm water that attract both trout and reds. Anglers who know where the "hot" flats are can often do very well in cold weather in relatively shallow water.

In spring, the fish again turn east and work their way down to the sounds. They spawn there in April and May, and again in September.

Biologists say that tagging studies indicate that most Georgia trout are hatched, live and die in the same estuary. Only five percent ever leave their home river, and scientists say this should make it possible to manage each estuary as a separate fishery as fishing pressure continues to increase.

At present, though, the trout numbers seem to be holding up well. The typical catch is fish from 12 to 15 inches (minimum legal size is 12 inches), which average 2 to 3 years old here.

"We may be seeing a slow decline in 'gator trout due to increasing fishing pressure," says Woodward, "but so far the overall numbers seem to be just fine."

Interestingly, Georgia has no net harvest and no commercial hook-and-line harvest of trout, a fact that makes their liberal sportfishing limits possible.

Best Spots

All the rivers that meet the ocean in Georgia have some trout fishing. The mouth of the Satilla and St. Andrews Sound are good, as are the waters around St. Simons Island. Altamaha Sound near the town of Darien is also very strong, as is Sapello Sound. The mouths of the Ogeechee and Savannah rivers also produce very well--in short, the entire coast has excellent trout fishing, and Georgia biologists say more trout are landed here per mile of shoreline than anywhere else in the nation--this, despite fishing pressure that would be seen as very modest in more populous areas.

Runs of trout occasionally show along the beaches of the Outer Banks of North Carolina. Most anglers use lures too large for the trout, since they're after stripers and jumbo blues, but a small plug or jig often connects with sizable trout.

Of course, the Georgia coast offers a lot more than just trout fishing. The coastal islands are among the most beautiful anywhere, and some like Cumberland have unique populations of wild horses. Some of the islands also offer superb deer hunting, and it's possible to combine a deer/trout trip in late fall--check the game commission for quota permit regulations. Jeckyll Island is the historic winter hideaway of turn-of-the-century millionaires, and a visit there today will tell you why. The area offers beauty, seclusion and outstanding sport--a great getaway.

South Carolina

The waters of South Carolina are much like that of Georgia says guide Fuzzy Davis of Hilton Head, and fishing techniques are much the same.

"Look for the "little" tides," he says. "On the first and third quarters of the moon, the tides are only 6 1/2 feet, while they may be 10 feet on the new and full. Lower tide flow means clearer water, and that makes the trout bite."

Davis says that fishing gets prime in the bays and sounds in May and continues strong around bars and points there until October. The fish then gradually move inland, up the coastal rivers, as the water cools. Sometime in mid-December,

123

Bucktails are also effective when the fish are up the coastal rivers. Locals say the artificials work best when tides are minimal, allowing the water to clear.

when the water temperature drops below 58 degrees, the fish become nearly dormant, and fishing slows for several months.

Davis says that when the fish are up the rivers, they most often hang around creek mouths, particularly if there's a cutbank adjacent. Live oyster bars also hold fish, and so do docks, piers and bridges.

"They look for anywhere they can get out of that strong current," says Davis. "The big, deep holes don't hold them very often because the flow is too strong."

Davis says the cooler water of winter drops algae levels and clears the water, making jigs effective. Lime green, smoke and pink are all popular colors, curly-tails the popular style.

The average inside fish goes just under two pounds here, and the limit is 15 daily. For bigger fish, Davis sometimes voyages to artificial reefs up to three miles off the Atlantic beach, where pods of jumbo trout are often found.

Among the more productive spots are Calibogue Sound, Port Royal Sound and St. Helena Sound. Good rivers include the Chechessie, Colleton, Beaufort and May, and Skull Creek and Broad Creek are also very good. The best trout fishing is mostly from Georgetown southward, because there are few sounds and river entries north of there. Hilton Head is the premiere resort location on the coast, with all the amenities and accommodations at all levels, plus quick access to good fishing.

North Carolina/Virginia

The sounds of North Carolina and Virginia are the northernmost limit of good spotted seatrout populations, and the fishing is distinctly seasonal, dropping to nothing in mid-December and staying that way until the waters warm back into the 60's in spring.

However, as with northern populations of many species, some of the biggest of the strain are found here. The all-tackle record, an unimaginable 16-pounder, was caught at Mason's Beach, Virginia in 1977.

The bays and sounds here are less murky than those of the Georgia and South Carolina coasts, and thus more productive for a variety of artificial lures, including jigs and slow-sinking plugs. Some areas support grass flats somewhat like those in Florida, and produce fine trout fishing from spring through fall.

In North Carolina, both Pamlico Sound and Albemarle Sound have seasonally good seatrout action. The fish go well up the Neuse, Pamlico and Pungo rivers in late fall, and are caught on the points and bars of the sounds in April, May and

Docks and piers form refuges from high current flow for South Carolina's coastal trout. Live shrimp is the favored bait.

June and again in September and October. In general they're found around areas with broken shoreline and depths of 2 to 7 feet.

Roanoke Sound and Croatan Sound are also productive, not only for trout but also for striped bass or "rockfish"

There are also runs of big trout along the beaches during summer and fall, with most fish caught in holes blown out close to the surf along Hatteras Island.

Chesapeake Bay is the last stronghold of seatrout along the Atlantic Coast, with the lower bay productive in summer, and the lower Rappahannock and York Rivers good in fall.

CHAPTER 18

GRASS ROOTS CONSERVATION

Flats anglers are dedicated to getting flats boats to run shallower so that they can penetrate further into those secret grass flats and mangrove sloughs where the big trout, snook and reds hide, but it's perhaps time now to think about the possible impact of this pursuit which so many of us have taken up in recent years.

Flats fishing, like turkey hunting, is a sport that can't be enjoyed by the masses, at least not without some sagacious controls.

By their very nature, flats are delicate parts of the estuarine environment, where ever they are found, from the Laguna Madre of Texas to the back side of the Chandeleurs in Louisiana to the big bays and sounds of Florida and the Carolinas.

In all of those areas, the reason there are trout, redfish and many other species is that the grass provides the base of a natural chain that not only nurtures and hides juveniles, but also grows tons of food to feed them.

Take away the grass and the fish disappear as well, as has been abundantly proven in highly-developed Florida estuaries such as Tampa Bay. Forty four percent of historic grass flats there have been destroyed, mostly by pollution and murky water, and fishing for grass-dependent species like trout is off at least 90 percent from historic levels.

When there were only a few flats anglers, the fact that they cut an occasional prop trail through a flat made little difference, and in fact might have been helpful, providing a bit of extra hiding area on low tides.

Shallow draft flats boats provide access to miles of great seatrout water--but anglers must learn to run responsibly and avoid grass damage if the areas are to remain open.

Grass Under Attack

But these days, with flats boats zipping every which way on weekends, joined by waves of jet skis and commercial net fishermen running tunnel boats and bait shrimpers dragging trawls in some regions, the impact is beginning to show. Some flats now have deep wheel tracks, the results of dozens of boats traveling the same route. The grass is not only clipped off, but plowed out roots and all. The results will take years to heal, say biologists, even if all traffic through the areas were stopped immediately.

Further, prop tracks tend to change the very nature of water flow over a flat. In areas of high tide flow, the tracks can initiate underwater erosion, which soon cuts the channel far wider and deeper than that created by the boats. More water volume then funnels through the cut, reducing the flow across the adjacent flats.

The result, in many cases, is reduced productivity of the entire area.

Frequent passage of boats through knee-deep water can also be a form of harassment of the fish that gather there, continuously chasing them from one area to another,

Large trout will abandon grass flats with high traffic areas. (Photo by Larry Larsen.)

preventing rest and effective feeding, blowing out schools of baitfish from their normal travel patterns.

The mud and broken grass stirred up by fast-moving outboards also contribute to turbidity of the water, which makes it more difficult for the surviving grass to survive, more difficult for new grass to take root. Light penetration is a chief determinant in the health of sea grasses, since they depend on sunshine to drive the photosynthesis cycle within them to create food from nutrients in the water.

Time To Police Ourselves

Scott Deal of Maverick Boats, one of the prime flats boat builders, believes that it's up to the industry to police itself before it is policed from the outside.

"We know that a boat run carelessly through the grass has a bad impact on the environment," says Deal. "It's up to us to educate the public to operate their boats in a way that doesn't destroy this habitat." Deal has been a stalwart supporter of the Florida Conservation Association as part of his efforts, and also sponsors annual flats fishing shows with strong conservation themes.

In Tampa Bay, the policing has already begun. A two-mile section along the northwest shore of Weedon Island has been closed to outboards, in part to protect manatees, but also as an effort to cut down destruction of the grass.

One of the prime movers of the effort was fishing guide and noted glass sculptor Russ Sirmons of St. Petersburg.

"On weekends, that area had become unfishable because there were so many boats blasting through there, and the water was being turned to muck. If you managed to find a redfish or a snook, you couldn't pole within range before some yahoo blew past at 40 miles an hour and spooked it."

Under the new rules, only trolling motors or push poles are allowed for propulsion in the closed areas. Sirmons and others say that the flat has become a refuge area, producing better fishing than ever before because fish gather there to avoid disturbance common in other areas. The result has not only pleased anglers, but attracted the attention of conservationists looking for ways to preserve grass beds without negatively impacting water recreation. Similar closed areas are already in the works for other parts of Tampa Bay.

However, when large flats are closed to outboards, anglers are effectively locked out since access to much of the backcountry depends on high speed "flats hopping" to reach those secret potholes and deep creeks where fish often gather. Some of this has already been put in place by folks with good intentions but perhaps not such a good idea of what makes up manatee habitat along the east coast of Florida. There, miles of 2-foot-deep water that would never float a seacow is off limits as manatee refuges, with a resulting crash in recreational use of the areas, at no benefit whatever to manatees.

Saving The Flats For Fishermen

What can you do to prevent destruction of grass beds and possibly more areas closed to outboards?

Run your boat sensibly. Know exactly how much water your boat can handle, and don't attempt to jump shallow, grassy flats where you know skeg or prop will cut into the bottom. Either seek a bare sand route into the area you want to fish, or shut down the outboard and go in by push pole or trolling motor.

An electric trolling motor is a great help in accessing the shallows without damaging the grass. Push poles also do the job.

Secondly, be aware of your wake--don't plow along in a bog when passing through a narrow channel inside the flats, because the resulting wake will help erode the shallows and make the water more murky.

And rig your boat right, so that the prop rides as high as possible, making minimal bottom contact. This includes either a mechanical or hydraulic jack plate to vertically lift the motor to minimal operating position, a lifting wing or hydrofoil on the cavitation plate to help with rapid planing, and on many boats, trim tabs to assist in a quick hole shot and a flat running attitude.

Using a relatively low-pitched prop will also help with quick hole shots that don't damage the bottom, as will use of a four-blade prop rather than a three. The new "shifting" props are also very helpful for quick takeoffs without bottom contact--Torque-Shift and Mercury both have shifting designs.

Rig your boat right and run it wisely. Prop, skeg, lower unit--and the flats themselves--will last longer.

133

CHAPTER 19

TROUT GUIDES

The following is by no means a complete list of trout guides, but it represents a sampling of some of the best from many top trout areas throughout the southeast.

One of the unusual aspects about guided trout trips is that it's common for the guide to fish right along beside his clients. He does this because his full attention to the boat may not be needed, in cases where you're drifting deep grass, and more importantly, because a lure that works just right is often needed to locate a school and give him time to get the anchor set. Since he's hopefully better at it than you are, he "samples" the water as you drift to make sure you're not missing the fish.

This is not to say you ought to accept a guide who shoulders you out of the way and catches your limit for you, by any means. But don't be concerned if you occasionally see an extra lure landing out there next to yours.

Rates range from $100 to $275 per day, including the boat and usually tackle and bait, though those who use lots of shrimp may require that you pay for what is used. Most guides use small boats for trout fishing, so limit their load to two or three, at most four anglers.

Many guides will also arrange accommodations at nearby hotels or fish camps if you book several days with them. The fish belong to you, not to the boat, but if the guide cleans them for you, it's customary to offer him an added tip, on top of the usual, for taking care of this job.

Everett Antrim, Port Richey, FL (813) 868-5747
Doug Bird, Corpus Christi, TX (512) 937-3589
Larry Blue, St. Petersburg, FL (813) 595-4798
Jim Bradley, Weeki Wachee, FL (904) 596-5639
Herb Brown, Tarpon Springs, FL (813) 797-2731
Frank Catino, Satellite Beach, FL (407) 779-9054
Charlie Cleveland, Tampa, FL, (813) 935-0241
Fuzzy Davis, Hilton Head, SC, (803) 671-1111
Ray DeMarco, Anna Maria, FL, (813) 778-9215
Corby Dolar, Homestead, FL, (305) 248-8712
Al Dopirak, Crystal Beach, FL, (813) 785-7774
Mike DuClon, Tarpon Springs,FL (813) 937-9737
Eric Ersch, Satellite Beach, FL, (407) 779-9054
Shawn Foster, Cocoa Beach, FL, (407) 784-2610
Ad Gilbert, Venice, FL, (813) 484-8430
Pete Greenan, Boca Grande, FL, (813) 923-6095
Ronnie Gronier, Venice, LA, (504) 534-9357
Paul Hawkins, St. Petersburg, FL, (813) 894-7345
Richard Howard, Clearwater, FL, (813) 446-8962
Van Hubbard, Boca Grande, FL, (813) 697-6944
Mike Locklear, Homosassa, FL, (904) 628-2602
Dave Markett, Tampa Bay FL, (813) 962-1435
Tim McOsker, St. Petersburg, FL, (813) 867-2544
Larry Mendez, Charolotte Harbor, FL, (813) 874-3474
Bill Miller, Charlotte Harbor, FL, (813) 935-3141
Chris Mitchell, Boca Grande, FL, (813) 964-2887
Scott Moore, Cortez, FL, (813) 778-3005
Abbie Napier, Cedar Key, FL, (904) 543-5511
Terry Parsons, Sebastian, FL (407)589-7782
Danny Patrick, Georgia coast, (904) 744-9534
Bill and Anna Rae Roberts, Cedar Key, FL (904) 543-5690
Dennis Royston, Hudson, FL, (813) 863-3204
Frank Schiraldi, Crystal River, FL, (813) 795-5229
Kenny Shannon, Boca Grande/Venice, FL, (813) 497-4876
Terry Shaughnessy, Hackberry, LA, (318) 762-3391
Russ Sirmons, St. Petersburg, FL, (813) 526-2092
Tim Slaught, Homosassa, FL (904) 628-5222
Tom Tamanini, Tampa Bay, FL, (813) 581-4942
Gilbert Vella, Port Isabel, TX, (512) 761-2865
Johnny Walker, Sarasota, FL, (813) 922-2287

Guides stay in touch with seasonal migrations of trout in their area, and can quickly put you on both large numbers of fish, and in the right season, gator-size trophies. They also have boats rigged right to reach the best waters in their region.

137

Earl Waters, Homosassa, FL, (904) 628-0333
Jay Watkins, Rockport, TX, (512) 729-9596
Mike Williams, Galveston, TX, (713) 723-1911
Bruce Williams, Crystal River, FL (904) 795-7302
Bryan Wolf, Corpus Christi, TX, (512) 643-8056
James Wood, Terra Ceia, FL (813) 722-8746

CHAPTER 20

TROUT COOKERY

The spotted seatrout just looks like it ought to taste wonderful, and it doesn't disappoint. It is among the most delicate and delightful of the sea's treats, never strong, never tough, good in every imaginable receipt. Trout are one of the few fish that don't become inedible in the largest sizes, and also one of the few which don't hide a nasty taste in their skins. They are, in short, the perfect table fish.

There are, however, a few unreconstructed Southerners who don't like trout. The charges are that they are soft, bland and without character--sort of like Democratic presidential candidates, some might say. (OK, some say that about Republican candidates.)

The secret, if there is one, is to treat trout with the respect their remarkable table qualities deserve--that is, to get them on ice immediately when caught, to clean them immediately when you return to the dock, and to store the filets promptly and properly in your freezer. It's true that trout quality degrades more quickly than firmer fish such as redfish or snook, but handled right they're great.

Best way to handle the fish on the water is to put a large, extra-thick garbage bag in your ice chest on top of a layer of ice, and deposit each fish in the bag as it's caught. That way, you don't get slime and blood on the drinks, and don't have a stinky mess in the chest when you're done, but the fish are chilled quickly.

Avoid putting trout on a stringer or in a live well--they die quickly, and the flesh soon starts to deteriorate.

139

Cleaning Trout

Trout are very easy to clean, requiring only a quick sweep down each side with a thin, sharp fillet knife to take off the filets. The rib bones are thin and are easily nipped with the sweep of the knife.

Start the cut right behind the gill plates and work the knife right down the backbone to just ahead of the tail--but don't cut through the tail skin if you prefer your fillets without the skin.

Simply turn the fillet over, use the carcass as a handle, and run the knife blade between the skin at the tail and the fillet. Work it against the cutting board back toward the head-end of the fillet to strip off the skin.

On all but the largest fish, it makes sense to cut out the rib cage and its bones in one slice, leaving a completely boneless chunk of flesh ready for the pan. On large fish, you may want to save the rib cage area and let diners pick out the bones as they go, since there's quite a bit of meat in this area on fish of 3 pounds and up.

If you like to fry your fish with the skin on (it's delicious) omit the skinning step and instead scrape down the skin with a teaspoon to get rid of slime and scales. This is easiest before you remove the fillets.

Parasites

Before we go on, we must touch on an indelicate topic. Worms.

There's nothing else to call them, and if you look at most trout fillets, you'll see a few of these white, threadlike critters winding through the meat. They look awful; soft, gummy eyeless creatures--and seeing one in a slice of trout is enough to turn off a lot of people to a trout dinner, especially if they haven't been standing close enough to the beer cooler.

There are two approaches. You can either cut the critters out--which wastes a lot of meat and a lot of time--or you can ignore them.

I ignore them.

Cooked, they become part of the flavor of the fish--you'll never notice. Just don't mention them to your dinner guests.

A stringer full of trout fillets. Stringers are not the best way to preserve the delicate flavor of trout, however--ice the fish immediately for premier taste.

(The worms are not harmful to humans and will not parasitize your mother-in-law, unfortunately.)

Freezing

Most people who think they don't like trout have been turned off by fish that were frozen improperly. You can't simply wrap trout fillets in foil and toss them in the freezer-- they become dry and flaky in only a few weeks.

The best technique is to put meal-sized portions into double-thick, locking freezer bags, add enough water to cover the flesh, and then burp out any remaining air before zipping the bag shut.

Label and date the bags and freeze immediately, and you'll find that the fillets will taste as good 12 months from now as they did yesterday. The water seals away any possibility of freezer burn and keeps the natural juices intact, preserving the quality long term.

(When you thaw the package, let it set for a few hours in the refrigerator so the ice will soften, then quick-thaw it under cool water from the faucet. Allowing the water to melt slowly while the fillets set in that water for a long period will soften the flesh and leach out the taste.)

141

Southern Fried Trout

Though a lot of us are getting away from fried foods these days, there's no question that one of the prime ways to handle trout is by frying. The flesh is so light and oil-free that it makes a particularly tasty treat when fried.

One of the best approaches is to cook it much like Cracker hunters prefer their wild turkey breast, deep fried.

For this one, cut the trout fillets into boneless two-inch squares, skins on, and drop them into a bag with flour or cornmeal, or both, seasoned with salt, pepper and garlic powder. (Shake-and-Bake fish coating is also good.) Shake until the pieces are coated.

Meantime, heat up a pot of vegetable oil to the smoking stage. (Drop a bit of flour in to test the heat--it should sizzle and turn brown almost instantly.) Best way to deep fry is outside on a propane burner like the rigs put out by Windy Cookers and others, so you keep the smell and the mess out of the house. The commercial cookers also have wire baskets that make it quick and easy to get the goodies in and out.

Put the trout pieces into the hot oil and let them fry until the coating just turns brown. Don't go off to get a beer while you're waiting--it only takes a few minutes, and if you overcook they're not good. Raise them clear and let them drain on paper towels before serving. You might want to toss some hush puppies in the hot oil while you're at it, to serve up on the side.

Whole Baked Trout

If you catch a whopper that you just can't stand to cut up for the pot before everybody sees it, you might consider baking it whole.

Gut the fish, remove the gills, and wash the body cavity thoroughly. Scrub the skin with a kitchen brush and water to get rid of slime and scales.

Put fresh orange sections, skins on, inside the body cavity to add a tang and scent. Score the skin, and squeeze some orange juice over these areas as well.

Wrap the fish in aluminum foil and place in a large cooking pan. Place the pan in a 350-degree oven and let it set through about half a six-pack. Remember, oven temperatures and

Anglers of the future may not string heavy catches like this one, but proper management can maintain stocks of big fish for catch-and-release action that remains strong indefinitely.

drinking times vary, so check it regularly after the first 40 minutes. A five-pounder will take somewhere between 60 and 90 minutes in most ovens. You know it's done when a fork penetrates easily all the way through near the shoulders.

Serve it up with plenty of parsley around the sides--and if you have a flair for the dramatic, stick a big silver Zara Spook in the mouth.

Baked Trout Fillets

Another good baking receipt makes use of skinned fillets. Again, line a cooking pan with aluminum foil before adding the fillets. The foil keeps the sticky mess out of the cookery, making cleanup easy.

Mix a can of condensed mushroom soup with half a can of milk and pour the mixture over the fillets. Then add some fresh sliced mushrooms and finely chopped onions on top of the fillets. If you're not on a diet, a topping of mozzarella or Parmesan cheese is a nice final touch.

Bake in a 350-degree oven until the fillets flake, maybe 30 minutes--check frequently and again, don't overcook. Dredge

143

the finished cuts out with a spatula so they don't break up, and serve with the pan drippings ladled over top. Wonderful stuff. (Did you ever notice how you can cook danged near anything under mushroom soup and it comes out great?)

CHAPTER 21

TROUT BIOLOGY AND CONSERVATION

Spotted seatrout grow fast, live hard and die young.
Not a bad way to go.

They reach spawning age quickly and mate year around,
though the peaks are from April through September in most
areas. Mike Murphy, biological administrator for the Florida
Department of Natural Resources, says that most male trout
reach sexual maturity by age 1 at a length of 9 to 12 inches,
while 50 percent of females are mature at 12 inches and age
1, and 90 percent are mature at 16 inches around age 2.

Growth Rates

In general, the females begin to outgrow the males after
their first birthday, says Murphy, although overall growth
rates vary considerably in different areas of the coast.

Trout grow fastest in the warmer months, and slow or stop
growing in the coldest months. This causes an "annulus" or
growth ring to form on the scales, just as rings on a tree stump
mark its age, and this along with microscopic examination of
the ear bones is the evidence scientists use to determine age.

Males average 12-13 inches at age 1, 14 inches at age 2 and
15 inches at age 3. The largest and oldest males studied were
found in the Indian River, with some reaching 25 inches at age
8, and weighing up to 5 pounds.

The DNR researchers found that females averaged 13
inches and from .5 to .8 pounds at age 1, 16-18 inches and 1-
2 pounds at age 2 and 19-22 inches and 2-3 pounds at age 3.
The largest and oldest females were again found in the Indian

River, where some were recorded at a length of 33 inches, a weight of 13 pounds and an age of 8 years. The following tables, from Florida DNR research, show further examples of length and weight increases.

TOTAL LENGTH (inches)						
AGE	Charlotte		Indian River		Apalachicola	
	M	F	M	F	M	F
1	12.3	13.0	13.2	13.8	11.8	13.6
2	13.6	16.3	14.8	18.0	14.0	17.6
3	14.8	18.9	16.4	21.6	15.6	21.1
4	16.1	21.1	18.1	24.7	16.8	24.1
5	17.3	22.9	19.7	27.4	----	26.8
6	18.6	24.4	21.4	29.7	----	29.2
7	----	25.7	23.0	31.7	----	----
8	----	26.7	24.6	33.4		

Note how the males disappear after age 4 in Apalachicola Bay, and after age 6 in Charlotte, but continue through age 8 in Indian River where biologists believe there may be a slightly different strain of "super trout" given to extended life span and rapid growth. The differences in weight are also obvious.

WEIGHT (pounds)						
AGE	Charlotte		Indian River		Apalachicola	
	M	F	M	F	M	F
1	0.4	0.5	0.7	0.8	0.5	0.8
2	0.6	1.1	1.0	1.9	0.9	1.8
3	0.8	1.9	1.4	3.3	1.2	3.0
4	1.1	2.9	1.9	5.1	1.5	4.5
5	1.4	3.9	2.6	7.0	--	6.2
6	1.8	4.9	3.3	9.0	--	7.9
7	--	5.8	4.2	11.0	--	--
8	--	6.7	5.2	13.0	--	--

Female trout grow faster and larger than males, and are more susceptible to being caught on hook and line. The largest trout strain is found in the Indian River, on Florida's East Coast.

Interestingly, Murphy points out, the differences in growth rate have an impact on managing trout through length limits. Limits which allow harvest of only large fish tend to reduce the take of males and increase the harvest of females because there are more large females in an unfished population.

Angling Mortality

Murphy also notes that females are more frequently caught by anglers. Fishing causes only about 46 percent of the conditional mortality in Charlotte Harbor for male trout, but is the end of 80 percent of the females. Natural mortality for females is about 26 percent, while natural causes kill about 33 percent of the males.

Trout are harvested heavily throughout the state. In Charlotte Harbor, scientists estimate that somewhere between 5 and 30 percent of the adult spawning stock survives compared to an unfished population. In Indian River Lagoon the survival is 10 to 15 percent, and in Apalachicola only 7 to 10 percent.

What this seems to tell us is that we are overfishing the stocks, if we want the sort of action on seatrout that was

The simple pleasures of trout fishing should remain available for anglers into the 2000's, so long as anglers insist on clean water and good management.

common in days gone by. The dramatic return of redfish to the shallows of Florida are clear evidence that tight harvest management and gamefish status are effective tools for restoration, but it takes a few years of everybody biting the bullet--zero or very low harvest--for the stocks to bounce back.

Of course, catch-and-release fishing may not be the answer in seatrout management, because they are among the most delicate of inshore fish. Many that are released, even after gentle handling, go belly up on the bottom, particularly in the warmer months. (There have been studies in Texas indicating that most trout survive, but virtually all experienced anglers in Florida agree that a lot of released trout don't make it.) Thus, it's likely that large minimum size laws may actually add to trout mortality, since some anglers will catch 50 to 100 undersized trout while trying for their 10 legal ones. Discussions on the depth of the problem, and its solution, are now underway in Florida's Marine Fisheries Commission. One possible way to reduce fishing morality is to allow anglers to keep the first 10 fish they catch, no matter what the size--

148

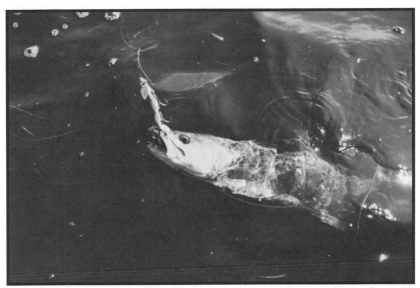

One possible way to reduce fishing morality is to allow anglers to keep the first 10 fish they catch, no matter what the size--or the first five, assuming we'll soon get a more restrictive limit to improve the stocks.

or the first five, assuming we'll soon get a more restrictive limit to improve the stocks.

Presumably, anglers with their limit on trout will then go off to pursue reds or snook or other species. Using de-barbed hooks also helps trout survival greatly, as does quick but gentle handling, using the grip that immobilizes trout, with the thumb and forefinger slipped just under the gill plates from the back.

Spawning

The primary spawning months in Charlotte Harbor were May through August. In the Indian River the peak months were April through August, with some activity into September. And in Apalachicola the strong peak is in May, with moderate activity through August.

In general, spawning starts when water temperature reaches about 75 degrees. If the inshore waters exceed 86, spawning usually stops. (Water temperatures in excess of 93 degrees are known to kill trout, and large numbers also die sometimes when the flats are rapidly chilled by a fast-moving freeze. Trout can survive water temperatures into the lower 50's if the drop is gradual, but a sudden drop within a few hours often shocks them and causes large kills, particularly in the Laguna Madre area of Texas where "Blue Northers" come sweeping down the plains with some regularity.)

One female may drop upwards of one million eggs in channels and holes adjacent to broad reaches of shallow grass. The eggs float so long as the salinity remains high, and optimum survival is at around 28 parts per thousand--thus, early hurricanes can do damage to a year-class by flushing the spawning areas with excessive fresh water.

Scientists Bill Semans, Jr. and Darlene Johnson, who prepared a trout study for the U.S. Fish and Wildlife Service, say most actual spawning is at night, when large numbers of fish aggregate and mill together, the males drumming softly.

The fertilized eggs hatch into larval fish after about 18 hours. Length at this point is about 1.3 to 1.6 mm, or around .06 inch long, and the fish are mostly controlled by the tides. They grow about 1 mm per week in the first summer, and by mid-summer they've reached 15 mm (.6 inch) and can control their motion by swimming--and most swim directly into the shallowest grass they can find, thus cementing the unbreakable relationship between preservation of grass beds and survival of seatrout. In their first winter, the young fish school up and move to deeper water, but will return to the grass as soon as spring arrives

Trout Travels

Trout don't migrate much more than this--they may travel several miles within an estuary to seek out temperature refuges in winter or food supplies at other seasons, but few ever leave the waters where they were hatched for good. Studies indicate that 95 percent of them never travel more than 30 miles from home. In the more northern portions of their range along the Atlantic Coast, they often move offshore in winter and return to the rivers and estuaries in spring, but throughout the Gulf and along Florida's southeast shore, they remain in the estuaries year around.

Trout don't migrate much --they may travel several miles within an estuary to seek out temperature refuges in winter or food supplies at other seasons, but few ever leave the waters where they were hatched for good.

Trout school most of their lives, but when females survive to age 6 or older, scientists have observed, they become solitary. (It's not clear whether this is by choice, or simply because there aren't many survivors from a school by age 6. Trout tend to school by size, and while there are abundant fish in the smaller lengths, those of age 6--2 feet long and weighing 6 pounds or better--are scarce.)

It's rare to catch big ones in exactly the same waters where the little ones are hitting. However, at times pods of small trout may be found close to pods of considerably larger ones, since both are attracted to the same habitat and feeding conditions. So, when you catch little ones, the biologists suggest, explore the area a bit and you may catch big ones as well.

Biologists have found that trout can stand salinities from 37 parts per thousand to 0--which is to say they can handle anything from offshore waters to the headwaters of a spring-fed river where bass and bluegills share the pool. You won't see trout in these areas very often, to be sure, but on the

151

coldest days of winter, it's not uncommon to find seatrout settled into the spring boil of freshwater rivers like the Homosassa and the Chassahowitzka on Florida's west coast, and well inland in many other areas throughout their range.

Preferred Foods

Trout feed primarily on shrimp in their early years, but after they reach 12 inches they more frequently eat fish, and the fish they eat get bigger as the trout grow larger.

However, fish of all sizes tend to feed on any abundant food supply, thus Indian River fish feed on shrimp in summer and early winter, but switch to fish in late winter and early spring. The big ones also home in on the finger mullet population in early fall.

And on the west coast, the annual crop of scaled sardines make that a preferred source through spring and summer. Like most wild creatures, seatrout take targets of opportunity, trying to get their nourishment with the least possible expenditure of energy, while at the same time avoiding becoming dinner themselves in the endless food chain of the sea.

Trout Fishing In The Future

Americans have awakened to the value of clean water and wild fish. Much has been lost, much that can never be restored or recovered. But the methods of modern marine fish management are becoming established and the public has shown themselves willing to support good management, both politically and financially. The seatrout should remain an abundant resource into the next millenia, so long as humans continue to enjoy the blessings the planet has bestowed, and remain willing to defend them.

FISHING & HUNTING
RESOURCE DIRECTORY

If you are interested in more productive fishing and hunting trips, then this info is for you!

Larsen's Outdoor Publishing is the publisher of several quality Outdoor Libraries - all informational-type books that focus on how and where to catch America's most popular sport fish, hunt popular and exciting big game, camp, dive or travel to exotic destinations.

The perfect-bound, soft-cover books include numerous illustrative graphics, line drawings, maps and photographs. The BASS SERIES LIBRARY as well as the HUNTING LIBRARIES are nationwide in scope. The INSHORE SERIES covers coastal areas from Texas to Maryland and foreign waters. The OUTDOOR TRAVEL SERIES and the OUTDOOR ADVENTURE LIBRARY cover the most exciting destinations in the world. The BASS WATERS SERIES focuses on the top lakes and rivers in the nation's most visited largemouth bass fishing state.

All series appeal to outdoorsmen/readers of all skill levels. The unique four-color cover design, interior layout, quality, information content and economical price makes these books hot sellers in the marketplace. Best of all, you can learn to be more successful in your outdoor endeavors!!

153

INSHORE SERIES

by Frank Sargeant

IL1. THE SNOOK BOOK

"Must" reading for anyone who loves the pursuit of this unique sub-tropic species. Every aspect of how you can find and catch big snook is covered.

IL2. THE REDFISH BOOK

Packed with expertise from the nation's leading redfish anglers and guides, this book covers every aspect of finding and fooling giant reds. You'll learn secret techniques revealed for the first time.

IL3. THE TARPON BOOK

Find and catch the wily "silver king" along the Gulf Coast, north through the mid-Atlantic, and south along Central and South American coastlines. Experts share their most productive techniques.

IL4. THE TROUT BOOK

You'll learn the best seasons, techniques and lures in this comprehensive book. Entertaining, informative reading for both the old salt and rank amateur.

BASS WATERS SERIES

by Larry Larsen

Take the guessing game out of your next bass fishing trip. The most productive bass water are described in this multi-volume series, plus ramp information, seasonal tactics, water characteristics and much more, including numerous maps and drawings and comprehensive index.

BW1. GUIDE TO NORTH FLORIDA BASS WATERS

From Orange Lake north and west.

BW2. GUIDE TO CENTRAL FLORIDA BASS WATERS

From Tampa/Orlando to Palatka.

BW3. GUIDE TO SOUTH FLORIDA BASS WATERS

From I-4 to the Everglades.

THE BASS SERIES LIBRARY
by Larry Larsen

1. FOLLOW THE FORAGE FOR BETTER BASS ANGLING VOL. 1 BASS/PREY RELATIONSHIP
Learn how to determine the dominant forage in a body of water, and you will consistently catch more and larger bass.

2. FOLLOW THE FORAGE FOR BETTER BASS ANGLING VOL. 2 TECHNIQUES
Learn why one lure or bait is more successful than others and how to use each lure under varying conditions.

3. BASS PRO STRATEGIES
Learn from the experience of the pros, how changes in pH, water temperature, color and fluctuations affect bass fishing, and how to adapt to weather and topographical variations.

4. BASS LURES - TRICKS & TECHNIQUES
Learn how to rig or modify your lures and develop specific presentation and retrieve methods to spark or renew the interest of largemouth!

5. SHALLOW WATER BASS
Learn specific productive tactics that you can apply to fishing in marshes, estuaries, reservoirs, lakes, creeks and small ponds. You'll likely triple your results!

6. BASS FISHING FACTS
Learn why and how bass behave during pre- and post-spawn, how they utilize their senses and how they respond to their environment, and you'll increase your bass angling success! This angler's guide to bass lifestyles and behavior is a reference source never before compiled.

7. TROPHY BASS
Take a look at geographical areas and waters that offer better opportunities to catch giant bass, as well as proven methods and tactics for man made/natural waters. "How to" from guides/trophy bass hunters.

8. ANGLER'S GUIDE TO BASS PATTERNS
Catch bass every time out by learning how to develop a productive pattern quickly and effectively. Learn the most effective combination of lures, methods and places for existing bass activity.

9. BASS GUIDE TIPS
Learn the most productive methods of top bass fishing guides in the country and secret techniques known only in a certain region or state that may work in your waters. Special features include shiners, sunfish kites & flies; flippin, pitchin' & dead stickin', rattlin', skippin' & jerk baits; deep, hot and cold waters; fronts, high winds & rain.

DEER HUNTING LIBRARY
by John E. Phillips

DH1. MASTERS' SECRETS OF DEER HUNTING
Increase your deer hunting success significantly by learning from the masters of the sport. New tactics and strategies.

DH2. THE SCIENCE OF DEER HUNTING
Specific ways to study the habits of deer to make your next scouting and hunting trips more successful. Learn the answers to many of the toughest deer hunting problems a sportsman ever encounters.

TURKEY HUNTING LIBRARY
by John E. Phillips

TH1. MASTERS' SECRETS OF TURKEY HUNTING
Masters of the sport have solved some of the most difficult problems you will encounter while hunting wily longbeardswith bows, blackpowder guns and shotguns.

OUTDOOR TRAVEL SERIES
by Timothy O'Keefe and Larry Larsen

Candid guides with vital recommendations that can make your next trip much more enjoyable.

OT1. FISH & DIVE THE CARIBBEAN - Volume 1
Northern Caribbean, including Cozumel, Caymans, Bahamas, Virgin Islands and other popular destinations.

OT3. FISH & DIVE FLORIDA & the Keys
Featuring fresh water springs; coral reefs; barrier islands; Gulf Stream/passes; inshore flats/channels and back country estuaries.

OUTDOOR ADVENTURE LIBRARY
by Vin Sparano

OA1. HUNTING DANGEROUS GAME
Know how it feels to face game that hunts back. You won't forget these classic tales of hunting adventures for grizzly, buffalo, lion, leopard, elephant, jaguar, wolves, rhinos and more!

LARSEN'S OUTDOOR PUBLISHING
CONVENIENT ORDER FORM
ALL PRICES INCLUDE POSTAGE/HANDLING

FRESH WATER
___ BSL1. Better Bass Angling Vol 1 ($13.95)
___ BSL2. Better Bass Angling Vol 2 ($13.95)
___ BSL3. Bass Pro Strategies ($13.95)
___ BSL4. Bass Lures/Techniques ($13.95)
___ BSL5. Shallow Water Bass ($13.95)
___ BSL6. Bass Fishing Facts ($13.95)
___ BSL7. Trophy Bass ($13.95)
___ BSL8. Bass Patterns ($13.95)
___ BSL9. Bass Guide Tips ($13.95)
___ CF1. Mstrs' Scrts/Crappie Fshng ($12.45)
___ CF2. Crappie Tactics ($12.45)
___ CF3. Mstr's Secrets of Catfishing ($12.45)
___ LB1. Larsen on Bass Tactics ($15.95)
___ PF1. Peacock Bass Explosions! ($16.95)
___ PF2. Peacock Bass & Other Fierce
　　　　Exotics ($17.95)

SALT WATER
___ IL1. The Snook Book ($13.95)
___ IL2. The Redfish Book ($13.95)
___ IL3. The Tarpon Book ($13.95)
___ IL4. The Trout Book ($13.95)
___ SW1. The Reef Fishing Book ($16.45)

OTHER OUTDOORS BOOKS
___ DL1. Diving to Adventure ($12.45)
___ DL2. Manatees/Vanishing ($12.45)
___ DL3. Sea Turtles/Watchers' ($12.45)
___ OC1. Outdoor Chuckle Book ($9.95)

REGIONAL
___ FG1. Secret Spots-Tampa Bay/
　　　　Cedar Key ($15.95)
___ FG2. Secret Spots - SW Florida ($15.95)
___ BW1. Guide/North Fl. Waters ($14.95)
___ BW2. Guide/Cntral Fl.Waters ($14.95)
___ BW3. Guide/South Fl.Waters ($14.95)
___ OT1. Fish/Dive - Caribbean ($11.95)
___ OT3. Fish/Dive Florida/ Keys ($13.95)

HUNTING
___ DH1. Mstrs' Secrets/ Deer Hunting ($13.95)
___ DH2. Science of Deer Hunting ($13.95)
___ DH3. Mstrs' Secrets/Bowhunting ($12.45)
___ DH4. How to Take Monster Bucks ($13.95)
___ TH1. Mstrs' Secrets/ Turkey Hunting ($13.95)
___ OA1. Hunting Dangerous Game! ($9.95)
___ OA2. Game Birds & Gun Dogs ($9.95)
___ BP1. Blackpowder Hunting Secrets ($14.45)

VIDEO &
SPECIAL DISCOUNT PACKAGES
___ V1 - Video - Advanced Bass Tactics $29.95
___ BSL - Bass Series Library (9 vol. set) $94.45
___ IL - Inshore Library (4 vol. set) $42.95
___ BW - Guides to Bass Waters (3 vols.) $37.95
Volume sets are autographed by each author.

BIG MULTI-BOOK DISCOUNT!
2-3 books, SAVE 10%
4 or more books, SAVE 20%

INTERNATIONAL ORDERS
Send check in U.S. funds; add $6
more per book for airmail rate

ALL PRICES INCLUDE POSTAGE/HANDLING

No. of books _____ x $_____ ea =$_____　　　*Special Package* _____ @ $_____
No. of books _____ x $_____ ea =$_____　　　*Video (50-min) $29.95* = $_____
　　Multi-book Discount (　%) $_____　　　　*(Pkgs include discount)= N/A*
　　　　SUBTOTAL 1　　$_____　　　　　　*SUBTOTAL 2*　　$_____

_____ **For Priority Mail (add $2 more per book)**　　$_____
TOTAL ENCLOSED (check or money order)　　$_____

*NAME*_____*ADDRESS*_____

*CITY*_____*STATE*_____*ZIP*_____

Send check or Money Order to: Larsen's Outdoor Publishing, Dept. 97-BK
2640 Elizabeth Place, Lakeland, FL 33813 (941)644-3381
(Sorry, no credit card orders)

WRITE US!

By the way, if your books have helped you be more productive in your outdoor endeavors, we'd like to hear from you. Let us know which book or series has strongly benefitted you and how it has aided your success or enjoyment.

We might be able to use the information in a future book. Such information is also valuable to our planning future titles and expanding on those already available.

Simply write to: Larry Larsen, Publisher, Larsen's Outdoor Publishing, 2640 Elizabeth Place, Lakeland, Fl 33813.

We appreciate your comments!

Save Money on Your Next Outdoor Book!

Because you've purchased a Larsen's Outdoor Publishing Book, you can be placed on our growing list of preferred customers.

● You can receive special discounts on our wide selection of Bass Fishing, Saltwater Fishing, Hunting, Outdoor Travel and other economically-priced books written by our expert authors.

PLUS...
● Receive Substantial Discounts for Multiple Book Purchases! And...advance notices on upcoming books!

Send in your name TODAY to be added to our mailing list

___ Yes, put my name on your mailing list to receive:

1. Advance notice on **upcoming outdoor books.**
2. Special **discount offers.**

Name_____

Address_____

City/State/Zip_____

**Send to: Larsen's Outdoor Publishing, Special Offers,
2640 Elizabeth Place, Lakeland, FL 33813**